"We are well familiar with the [illegible] and make disciples of all the nations...teaching them to observe all things that I have commanded you' (Matthew 28:19-20 NKJV), but what does that look like in our hearts, homes, families, and ministries? How can we be personally discipled, and how can we disciple others? Loving God is a thorough, practical answer to those questions. With the tender heart of a father and friend, Dr. McDill gently leads readers through a journey of discipleship—one you can travel for yourself and then extend to others in your sphere of influence. This book is filled with wisdom, actionable steps, and companion resources. It will deeply affect you the first time you read it, and then you will return to it time and again as a handbook for continuing your own discipleship and leading others into the abundant life of Christ as well. Parents, especially, will find useful and practical discipleship insight here. Loving God is a resource every believer should have!"

Dr. Dick Eastman
International President Every Home for Christ
Author of The Hour That Changes the World

"The Great Commission of Jesus Christ gives all of us who are disciples of Christ the responsibility to go and make disciples of others. We're to baptize the new disciples, and then, says Jesus, we're to begin 'teaching them to observe all that I commanded you.' The book in your hands is designed to help one disciple of Jesus teach other disciples about Jesus and about observing all that He commanded. It gives practical, biblical instruction for those wanting to be better followers of Christ as well as for those who want to help these disciples grow in Christlikeness. It can be especially useful for parents looking for resources to instruct their older children and teenagers in the ways of God.

Donald S. Whitney
Professor of Biblical Spirituality and Associate Dean for the School of Theology, the Southern Baptist Theological Seminary, Louisville, KY.
Author of Spiritual Disciplines for the Christian Life, Praying the Bible, and Family Worship

Loving God

Loving God

A PRACTICAL HANDBOOK FOR DISCIPLESHIP

Dr. Matthew McDill

ISBN-13: 9780692872215
ISBN-10: 0692872213

Contents

I am so grateful for the support of my wife, Dana, and our children;
for the encouragement and help from my church,Highland Christian Fellowship;
and for the faithful discipleship of my parents,
Wayne and Sharon McDill.

Forward

—∞—

For many years I have advised graduate students and teaching colleagues about their writing. Spurgeon told his students that the first requirement for a sermon is that you have something to say. I have borrowed that simple bit of wisdom and applied it to writing. Writing a book is hard work, but the first requirement is that you have something to say.

This book by my son, Matthew McDill, clearly reveals that he has something to say and that it took a lot of hard work to say it well. In a real sense this is his testimony. As young students in elementary school, Matthew and his sister Anna walked across the street to our home a half day every school week for "Wisdom Class."

Our school district in Oregon made provision for that half day as "time release" for religious instruction at home. Matthew's mother planned a challenging curriculum including biblical wisdom, Scripture memory, prayer, and basic disciplines for a follower of Christ. So today, with children of their own, Matthew and his sister pass along that same wisdom to their children.

Loving God is, as the title indicates, is *A Practical Handbook for Discipleship.* It combines a basic biblical understanding of the life of a disciple with very practical counsel as to how to apply the personal disciplines for that life. But it does not present a religious works view of the Christian life. Woven throughout the book is the underlying assurance of the grace that is ours in all that God provides in Christ.

Being a Christian is not basically about religion, or morality, or ritual, or doctrine. It is a matter of following Jesus in surrender to Him. A Christian disciple is a follower of Jesus. The focus of *Loving God* is that wonderful relationship we have with Him. By his grace, God has given us everything we need for life and godliness. He has also called us to respond to him with the discipline and faithfulness that expresses our love.

This book will be especially helpful for parents as a guide to discipling their children. It can provide a framework for understanding and study for any mentoring relationship. But we cannot teach what we do not know. Our children and students may well learn more from our example than from our lessons. So *Loving God* is first for me, and for you, as a helpful reminder of what it means to follow Jesus.

Wayne McDill
Southeastern Baptist Theological Seminary
Wake Forest, North Carolina
May 2017

Here is another book that God will use to encourage you, bless you, and challenge you. I know this statement is true because this book is based on the greatest book ever written, the Holy Bible, the book written by God! How amazing it is to me that I have had the privilege in my 75 years on this earth to come to know personally the Author of the greatest book ever written.

I also know personally, since even before his birth, the author of this book. I am his mother.

Since Jesus, the God Man, no longer walks this earth, it is no longer possible for me to know Him personally in the flesh, as I do my son. But by the awesome gift of God's Holy Spirit in me I can know *Him* through the Book He has written, His love letter to me. To know Him is to love Him. Getting to know God through His Book is the highest priority of my life.

How joyful it is for me to get to have a part by legacy in a book that explains in detail and practical application *Loving God*. Thank you, Matthew, for being obedient to the Holy Spirit's direction through the Holy Word of God to you to write this book. I am excited to get to use it to teach others how *Loving God* is the beginning of wisdom, purpose, peace, and true joy. This book is a gift to God's people through you, God's gift to our family.

Sharon McDill
Wake Forest, North Carolina
May 2017

INTRODUCTION

How to Use This Book

I KNOW VERY FEW CHRISTIANS who have been discipled well. By *discipled*, I mean that a person has been trained and led through the basic principles and disciplines of the Christian life. As a pastor and Bible teacher, I have spoken with many people about their relationships with God. We talk about things like purpose in life, spending time with God, learning how to pray, understanding God's Word, and living in victory over sin. We talk about engaging in personal ministry, developing family relationships, discerning God's will, and being organized, disciplined people. But I meet few Christians who feel like they have been intentionally taught and led through the biblical principles needed to succeed in these areas of life. The predominant feeling is this: "I want to follow God, but I'm not really sure how to do it."

If you are taking a look at this book, then this may be how you feel. Or you may be responsible for discipling others and need some help in knowing where to start. I would love to have a cup of coffee with you and talk about these things. That is how discipleship takes place—in the context of face-to-face relationships in everyday life. Since I can't do that with all of you, I am writing this book. I hope that it will help you learn to love God. But while books and other resources play important roles in your spiritual growth, they cannot replace face-to-face, real-life discipleship. The good news is that God has already put people in our lives to disciple us. He has given us dads and moms, husbands, pastors, older men and women, and friends to help us learn to follow Jesus.

"Yes, but they aren't doing it!" you might complain. I believe you. That is why we have a discipleship problem in the church. So what are we going to do about it? What are *you* going to do about it? We have to break this cycle of failing discipleship. *You* have to break the cycle. If your father or mother did not disciple you, you can choose to be the father or mother who does. If you have not had older men and women in your life to mentor you, you can choose to become a mentor.

I offer this book to you as a tool to break the cycle of failing discipleship. If you have not been discipled, then this is a great place to start. But be sure that you add the relational aspect of discipleship. Seek out an older man or woman you respect, and ask him or her to go through this handbook with you. Develop a small group of believers who can read it with you, or simply take the journey with a fellow believer who wants to grow.

If your father or mother did not disciple you, you can choose to be the father or mother who does.

If you are a parent who wants to disciple your children, then this book is for you. You will find here the information and tools necessary to lay a solid foundation for helping your children follow Jesus. For your younger children, you can communicate the concepts presented here in ways that they can understand. Your older children will be able to read through this book with you.

There are two more aspects of this book I would like to bring to your attention. First, I have made an effort to build all principles and practical applications on the truth of God's Word. There is *a lot* of Scripture here. It is often tempting for readers to skip quotes and Scripture references. Please resist this temptation. Each verse written out in this book is thoughtfully and intentionally placed there for you to read. When you get to the Bible verses, instead of skipping them, slow down and read them carefully. Here is your first opportunity. Jesus describes the central role and power of his Word in the life of his disciples:

If you abide in my word, you are truly my disciples,
and you will know the truth, and the truth will set you free.
John 8:31–32

The second aspect of this book I want to point out is that this is a *handbook*. It is not something you just read one time and put back on the shelf. It is more like a reference book that you can go back to regularly as you grow in your walk with Christ, develop the disciplines described here, and try to help others follow him, too.

The goal of discipleship and the purpose of this book is very well stated by Paul:

> *Him we proclaim,*
> *warning everyone and teaching everyone with all wisdom,*
> *that we may present everyone mature in Christ.*
> Colossians 1:28

CHAPTER 1

Finding Your Purpose

ONE DAY, WHEN SHOPPING AT Trader Joe's, I saw an employee carrying a sign that read, "Have a question? Ask me!" So I walked up to the young man and asked him, "What is the meaning of life?" He looked at me, surprised and speechless. When I broke into a grin, he was relieved and seemed to hope that I didn't actually expect him to answer the question. People often refer to this as the supremely difficult or unanswerable question. Is it really impossible to answer?

Like most people, you have probably asked yourself, "Why am I here?" Another way of putting it might be this: "What is the purpose of my life?" You can make up your own answer to that question, and many people do. However, many sense that there is a greater purpose outside of themselves to discover. Who or what else might determine our purpose in life? This brings us to another question that most people ask: "Where did I come from?"

We might begin answering this question with "From my mother and father." But where did they come from? Where did any of us come from? Where did the world come from? There are primarily two common answers to this question: We came from nothing (the Big Bang theory and evolution), or we came from God (some intelligent, powerful being). If we came from nothing, then you get to make up your own purpose in life (because there really isn't one). If we came from God, then we should find out what God's purpose is for us.

So which explanation makes more sense to you? Have we come from nothing or from God? It seems obvious to me that a world full of beauty, freedom, design, love, morality, and order did not come from nothing. The explanation that God created everything makes more sense to me. The Bible teaches that the existence of God is obvious to us because of creation.

For what can be known about God is plain to them, because God has shown it to them.
For his invisible attributes, namely his eternal power and divine nature,
are clearly perceived, ever since the creation of the world,
in the things that have been made. So they are without excuse.
Romans 1:19–20

How do we know who this Creator God is? God has not only revealed himself in creation but he has also revealed himself through the Bible. The Bible claims to be God's book to us.

All Scripture is breathed out by God and is profitable
for teaching, for reproof, for correction, and for training in righteousness,
that the man of God may be complete, equipped for every good work.
2 Timothy 3:16–17

But aren't there other gods and bibles? How do we know that the Christian Bible is the right one? You can read the Bible, compare it with other scriptures, and decide for yourself which one, if any, is from God. You will find that the Bible is internally coherent and confirmed by our experience in the world. This means that it is in agreement with itself and with what we learn from creation. You should not take another person's word for it. Read the Bible, and decide for yourself.

I am suggesting that these facts are obvious: (1) God created everything; and (2) the Bible is God's Word. So why are there so many other religions and world views? Are there really logical and scientific arguments against what the Bible teaches about God? In Romans 1, the apostle Paul explains why people reject God. He says that "by their unrighteousness," they "suppress the truth" (Rom. 1:18). He goes on:

For although they knew God, they did not honor him as God or give thanks to him,
but they became futile in their thinking, and their foolish hearts were darkened…
They exchanged the truth about God for a lie
and worshipped and served the creature rather than the Creator,
who is blessed forever! Amen.
Romans 1:21, 25

Yes, there are difficult questions about God, the world, and the Bible. But there are many reasonable and satisfying answers for those with open hearts and minds. Yes, what scientists say often seems to contradict what the Bible says is true. But "scientific" conclusions have changed throughout history. Everyone has his or her own bias, even a scientist. In addition, there are laws of nature and observations about the universe that point to the existence of God and his creation of everything.[1]

I know that some people are genuinely confused and want to know the truth. If they honestly seek the truth, they will find it. In the end, those who reject God do not do so based on scientific evidence or intelligent reasoning. They don't believe in God because they don't want to. They don't want to believe in God because they don't want to be accountable to him. They are not making a mental choice; they are making a moral choice.

God Gives You Purpose

If you have come to the conclusion that God exists and that he has revealed himself through the Bible, then we can answer the question, "Why am I here?"

I remember the day I discovered the simple and powerful answer. I was in college, sitting in a Sunday School classroom and reading the Bible before things got started. In the Bible story I was reading, an expert of the Jewish law asked Jesus a question: "Which commandment is the most important of all?" What an opportunity, and what a question! God had given the Jews hundreds of commandments in the Old Testament. Here is Jesus, God in the flesh, and he was asked to boil it all down to the most important commandment of all! His answer is no less amazing and satisfying. Jesus answered by quoting from Deuteronomy 6:4:

Hear, O Israel: The Lord our God, the Lord is one.
And you shall love the Lord your God with all your heart and with all your soul and with all your mind and with all your strength.
Mark 12:30

This is it. This is what God wants from us. God created us to have a personal, loving relationship with him. I'm not sure if I could have guessed what Jesus was going to say in answer to this question, but when I heard it, it answered the longings of my heart.

As I sat there in that Sunday School classroom as a nineteen-year-old young man, my life took on a new direction. I had grown up in church and heard the Bible taught my entire life. I had undoubtedly heard these verses before. But that morning, I *understood* them. I realized that I had been striving to "be a good Christian." I was failing to see that there was something greater than doing the right thing. Jesus severely criticized the Jewish teachers for knowing the Scriptures and keeping the law yet failing to do what God really wanted. They failed to love him.

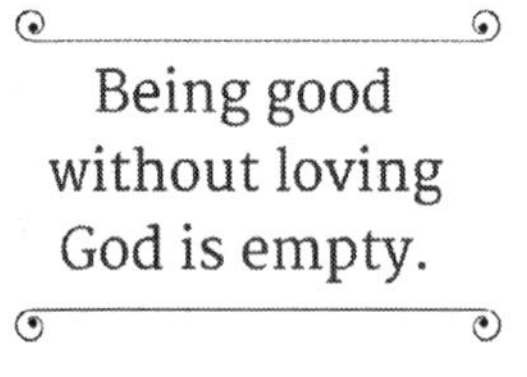
Being good
without loving
God is empty.

Hundreds of passages throughout the Bible reveal that God wants us to love him. The whole Bible, from beginning to end, speaks of God's relationship with man. We see it in God's relationship with the patriarchs; God's covenant with Israel and hatred of idolatry; the sending of his own Son to take our punishment and provide forgiveness; the personal, indwelling presence of God by his Spirit; and the fulfillment of all creation in the marriage supper of the Lamb, uniting Christ and his Bride, the Church.

When we discover that God's purpose for us is to love him, everything changes. *Why* we do what we do matters to God. We come to understand that being good without loving God is empty. Loving God is the real good, and it is in love that we find the joy and satisfaction of life.

Restoring Your Relationship with God

"Give Grandma a hug!" The toddler refuses, hiding behind Mom's legs. Now what? Mom is embarrassed about her child's behavior and feels bad for Grandma. Even worse, the little one has disobeyed her mom. Some parents proceed to give awkward public lectures or vain threats and bribes. Others swoop their child off to another room for discipline. The tear-streaked grandchild returns to give a reluctant hug.

How does Grandma feel about all this? "Leave her alone," she says. "It's all right. She'll give me a hug when she's ready." Does Grandma want a forced hug? Of course not. Grandma wants love, not just a hug. True love is freely given; you cannot force someone to love.

Since God created us to love him, he also created us with freedom of choice. We can choose to love and relate to God, or we can choose not to. When God created the first two humans, Adam and Eve, he gave them a choice. Since God wanted a loving relationship with them, he gave them the choice to trust and obey him or to do things their own way. Adam and Eve made the wrong choice. The Bible calls this failure to love and obey God *sin*. Sin has been a part of human life ever since.

Sin is the rejection of God and of what he says is good and right. God loves us, and what he tells us to do, or not to do, is good for us. God is truth and goodness and love. When he tells us to trust and love him only, he is doing what is best for us. He is giving us himself. What God tells us to do, or not to do, is not only good for us, but it is also right. He tells us to love others, which means that we do not lie to, steal from, or harm them. Everyone knows that this is right behavior.

All of us have failed to love God and do what is right. All of us have failed to love others. All of us have sinned.

All we like sheep have gone astray; we have turned—every one—to his own way.
Isaiah 53:6

All have sinned and fall short of the glory of God.
Romans 3:23

What do we do with people who steal from or harm others? Even people who don't believe in God believe in justice. This is why we have justice systems that punish people who commit crimes. Because of this, it is not difficult for us to understand God's standard that those who disobey his law must be punished. Much more than human laws, God's laws are good and right. So we can expect consequences and punishment for our sin. The Bible teaches that punishment for sin is eternal separation from God in hell.

Now, let's see where we stand. God created us to love him. He gave us a choice to love and obey him so that we might enjoy his life and goodness. However, all of us have chosen to disobey God instead of love him. We are therefore guilty of sin and deserve to be punished.

This is where the good news (the Gospel) comes in! God loved us so much that over two thousand years ago, he became a man, Jesus Christ, and died on a Roman cross to take the punishment for our sin. Then he came back to life and returned to heaven. You can read the whole story of Jesus from several perspectives in the Gospels of the New Testament (Matthew, Mark, Luke, and John). This rescue mission was God's plan all along. There are many prophecies about it in the Old Testament.

Surely he has borne our griefs and carried our sorrows;
yet we esteemed him stricken, smitten by God, and afflicted.
But he was pierced for our transgressions; he was crushed for our iniquities;
upon him was the chastisement that brought us peace, and with his wounds we are healed.
All we like sheep have gone astray; we have turned—every one—to his own way;
and the LORD has laid on him the iniquity of us all.
Isaiah 53:4–6

We were hopelessly separated from God and heading for eternal punishment. But God wouldn't have it. God is able to fulfill his purposes and has satisfied both love and justice. There is now a way to know and love God again. We must confess and repent of our sin, believe that Jesus Christ took the punishment for our sin, and receive by faith his forgiveness. Our choice remains. We turn back to God and receive Christ's payment for our sin, or we must pay for our own sin in hell, separated from God forever.

But [God] is patient toward you, not wishing that any should perish,
but that all should reach repentance.
2 Peter 3:9

Have you placed your faith in Jesus Christ for salvation? Have you restored your relationship with God through Christ and determined to love him? If you have not, do it now. Talk to God, and confess your sin to him. Express your faith that Christ paid for your sins on the cross. Express your desire to love and obey him for the rest of your life. Receive his forgiveness, and rejoice in his love!

Discussion Questions

- Which explanation makes more sense to you, that we came from nothing or from God?
- How has God revealed himself to us?
- How do we know that the Bible is from God?
- Why don't people believe in God?
- What is our purpose in life?
- What is sin?
- What are the consequences of sin?
- How do we receive forgiveness for our sin?

Big Ideas

- God has not only revealed himself in creation, he has also revealed himself through the Bible.
- The Bible is internally coherent and confirmed by our experience in the world.
- People don't believe in God because they don't want to. They don't want to believe in God because they don't want to be accountable to him.
- God created us to have a personal, loving relationship with him.
- Since God created us to love him, he also created us with freedom of choice.
- Sin is the rejection of God and of what he says is good and right. All of us have sinned.
- The Bible teaches that punishment for sin is eternal separation from God in hell.

- God loved us so much that over two thousand years ago, he became a man, Jesus Christ, and died on a Roman cross to take the punishment for our sin.
- We must confess and repent of our sin, believe that Jesus Christ took the punishment for our sin, and receive by faith his forgiveness.

For Further Reading

Baucham, Voddie. 2004. *The Ever-Loving Truth: Can Faith Thrive in a Post-Christian Culture?* Nashville: Broadman & Holman Publishers.

Geisler, Norman and Frank Turek. 2004. *I Don't Have Enough Faith to Be an Atheist*. Wheaton, Illinois: Crossway Books.

Lewis, C. S. 1980. *Mere Christianity*. New York: Macmillan Publishing Company.

CHAPTER 2

Giving It All

"WILL YOU MARRY ME?" THE young man on his knee looked up into her bright eyes.

She beamed and squealed, "Yes!"

"Great! Now, let's get one thing straight. I will be a faithful husband to you and love you all year long, as long as I can go out on just one date a year with another woman. Will that be all right?"

How would you guess the young lady responds? Most women I know would never agree to such an arrangement! The meaning and security of marriage is that we get our spouses all to ourselves. This is what we call the exclusivity of marriage. Everyone else is excluded from that special relationship.

WHAT GOD WANTS FROM US

The exclusivity of marriage helps us understand what God wants in our relationships with him. God has created us to love him. That is our purpose. The primary question of this book is this: "How do we love God?" The first way I want to answer this question is to explain the *scope* of loving God. In other words, how much of me and my life does loving God include? We can return to Jesus's words to discover the answer:

> *Hear, O Israel: The Lord our God, the Lord is one.*
> *And you shall love the Lord our God with all your heart and with all your soul and with all your mind and with all your strength.*
> Mark 12:30

What is the scope? How much of me and my life does loving God include?

All.

"All" is repeated in this verse four times. He wants us all to himself! "All" leaves nothing out.

Jesus shoots straight with us. He doesn't lure us into a deal and then reveal later in the fine print what is really required of us. When people tried to follow Jesus while he was here on earth, he wanted to make sure they understood what he expected from them.

And he said to all, "If anyone would come after me,
let him deny himself and take up his cross daily and follow me."
Luke 9:23

Now great crowds accompanied him, and he turned and said to them,
"If anyone comes to me and does not hate his own father and mother
and wife and children and brothers and sisters,
yes, and even his own life, he cannot be my disciple.
Whoever does not bear his own cross and come after me cannot be my disciple.
For which of you, desiring to build a tower, does not first sit down and count the cost,
whether he has enough to complete it...
So therefore, any one of you who does not renounce all that he has cannot be my disciple."
Luke 14:25–28, 33

Pretty extreme, isn't it? As soon as we consider following him, he tells us to count the cost. Again, the deal is total. Is that what you signed up for? Were you under a different impression of what it means to follow Jesus?

Instead of this radical, fulfilling life in relationship with God, many of us got a stingy, religious version of Christianity. Christianity is a religion, of course, according to the dictionary definition. But religion, in its broadest and usually most negative sense, is hollow. Religion allows you to focus on institutions, doctrines, dues, human leaders, ritual, and self-righteousness. Many religious people think they can give a *portion* of their lives to God. Many use religion to serve themselves and to make themselves feel better by trying to ease their consciences. American Christianity is often presented as a self-service program that will make one's life better.

What is your understanding of what it means to be a Christian? Maybe it is time for a reassessment. You must count the cost.

If you are going to follow Jesus, you cannot live for yourself. Jesus said that if you want to follow him, you must "deny yourself." Either Jesus will be in charge of your life, or you will. Either you will do what Jesus wants you to do, or you will do what you want to do. You cannot do both. We must lay down any of our own personal dreams and goals and seek God to know what he wants us to do with our lives.

We are naturally committed to keeping ourselves safe and comfortable. If you are going to follow Jesus, you must let go of this agenda. When he tells us to take up our cross, he is inviting us to join him in a life of redemptive suffering. This kind of suffering does not refer to the normal troubles of life we all encounter. It is the difficulty and consequence of living for Jesus in a world that is in rebellion against God. Jesus said:

> *You will be hated by all for my name's sake…*
> *And do not fear those who kill the body but cannot kill the soul.*
> *Rather fear him who can destroy both soul and body in hell.*
> Matthew 10:22a, 28

If you are going to follow Jesus, you cannot live for others. Jesus said that a person cannot be his disciple unless he hates "his own father and mother and wife and children." Since Jesus has told us to love others, especially our family members, we know that he doesn't really expect us to hate our families (Eph. 5:25; Titus 2:4). He is using extreme language to make the point that we must love God much, much more than anyone else.

We naturally want to be accepted, respected, and liked by others. Jesus is making it clear that we cannot be both people pleasers and Jesus pleasers. We often make decisions based on what will make people happy, what creates the most peace, or what will cause people to like us. As disciples of Jesus, our only concern is to follow him. There is no promise that this will result in the greatest number of happy people, the most relational peace, or maximum popularity.

> We cannot be both people pleasers and Jesus pleasers.

If you are going to follow Jesus, you must choose the path of redemptive suffering. When Jesus said that those who follow him must take up their cross daily, he had in mind his own crucifixion. Nailing people to a cross was the way that Romans executed criminals. So we know that the cross represents suffering. As we have already discussed, Jesus died to take the punishment for our sins. This was God's plan for offering us forgiveness. Therefore, the cross also represents redemption. When Jesus asks us to take up our cross and follow him, he is asking us to take up his mission of reconciling men to God. He is asking us to accept the path of self-sacrifice and suffering that this requires. There are many passages in the Bible that assure us that if we live for Christ, we will suffer for him (Matt. 10:16–39; John 15:18–25; 2 Tim. 3:12).

Suffering for Christ can be as minor as choosing to be disciplined and self-controlled in order to obey him. Suffering includes resisting sin and fighting in the spiritual battle. It includes the hard work that is necessary to serve Christ and fulfill his mission in the world. We will suffer as we experience trials, rejection, and persecution because we are following Christ. We may even be called upon to give our lives for him.

I think it is interesting that Jesus said we must take up our cross *daily*. Every day, we have the opportunity once again to take up Christ's mission of redemptive suffering. I like to imagine that we carry the cross through the day and then set it next to our beds as we go to sleep. When we wake up in the morning, it is there for us to pick up again…or not. Many mornings, I have walked right by the cross and instead have chosen to live for my own comfort and agenda.

The cost of all this sounds pretty steep, doesn't it? Why would anyone choose to follow Jesus?

What God Wants to Give Us

The kingdom of heaven is like treasure hidden in a field,
which a man found and covered up.
Then in his joy he goes and sells all that he has and buys that field.
Matthew 13:44

Why would a man sell all that he has to buy a field with a treasure in it? I can think of only one reason. The treasure in the field is worth more than all he has! While we are called to give *all* to Jesus, Jesus actually gives us *more* in return. The key to understanding this is remembering that this life is temporary. Jesus said:

Do not lay up for yourselves treasures on earth,
where moth and rust destroy and where thieves break in and steal,
but lay up for yourselves treasures in heaven, where neither moth nor rust destroys
and where thieves do not break in and steal.
For where your treasure is, there your heart will be also.
Matthew 6:19–21

One of the most important foundations to a Christian world view is to understand that God is eternal and spirit, and that this world is temporary and material. This is why faith is essential to the Christian life. Here is a definition of faith:

Now faith is the assurance of things hoped for, the conviction of things not seen.
Hebrews 11:1

Faith is confidence in things that haven't happened yet and in things we can't see. This is how we get the term "blind faith." "Blind faith" is used by the world to mean believing something without having any reason to do so. However, that is not the biblical meaning of faith. While the objects of faith are invisible, faith is based on good evidence and sound reasoning. As I have already mentioned, in Romans 1, Paul argues:

Romans 1 makes it clear that biblical faith is not blind faith. While the objects of faith are invisible, faith is based on good evidence & sound reasoning. God is clearly seen through the works of Creation. (Rom. 1:20)

For his invisible attributes, namely, his eternal power and divine nature, have been clearly perceived, ever since the creation of the world, in the things that have been made. So they are without excuse.
Romans 1:20

God is invisible, but we believe in him because of the clear evidence we see for his existence in creation.

So here is the deal he offers us. We give him our lives, all that we are and have, and he gives us eternal, spiritual life. We accept the necessary path of suffering because of sin in the world, and he gives his grace and presence in the midst of trouble. In this life he gives us joy, peace, purpose, and love. We also have hope in eternal peace and rest with him. We give him ourselves, and he gives us himself!

Getting Right with God

In the last chapter, we discussed how to place our faith in Jesus as Savior and Lord. The confession of the Christian is this: "Jesus is Lord!" (Rom. 10:9). When Jesus is Lord of your life, that means that he is in charge. There are two steps we can take to acknowledge the lordship of Jesus in our lives. The first is to remove sin from our lives. The second is to surrender every part of our lives to God in obedience.

Sin is the rejection of God and what he says is good and right. Once we have sinned, it must be paid for; there must be justice. Either we can take our own punishment, or we can let Jesus do it. The condition of allowing Jesus to pay for our sins is to confess our sin and repent. To confess our sin is to agree with God that what we did was wrong. To repent is to resolve to stop doing it, thus removing that sin from our lives.

Confessing our sin and repenting is not something we do only one time when we become a Christian. This is a regular part of the Christian life. We want to do our best to always be right with God and live in the fullness of the Holy Spirit. Paul writes:

And do not get drunk with wine, for that is debauchery, but be filled with the Spirit.
Ephesians 5:18

When Paul contrasts being drunk with being filled with the Spirit, he is helping us understand that he is talking about *control.* When we are controlled by wine, the result is debauchery. When we are controlled by the Spirit, the result is worship and submission (Eph. 5:19–21). Our responsibility is to surrender to the control and power of the Holy Spirit. When we find that we are not living in the fullness of the Holy Spirit, we can confess our sin and turn back to him.

Often Christians will go days, weeks, or even months without confessing their sins and getting right with God. After a long period of ignoring sin in your life, getting right with God may take some significant time alone with him. Once your sins are confessed and up to date, then it is easy to incorporate confession into your daily time with God.

Processing the sin in our lives can be overwhelming. It is important to understand that when we talk to God about our sin, we are having a conversation with our loving Father. He has adopted and accepted us based on the saving work of Jesus on the cross. We must be able to distinguish the loving, restorative conviction of our Father from the destructive accusations of Satan. Satan wants us to feel guilty for our sin and to draw away from God. He wants us to beat up on ourselves and refuse to forgive ourselves. If we fall into this trap, we have forgotten the Gospel! When our Father convicts us of sin, he is drawing us close to himself and calling us to forgiveness and freedom.

Another difficulty in processing our sin is the discouragement that comes when we keep repeating sinful behavior. We often feel like failures, dirty and unworthy. It is as though we have fallen in the mud *again* and just want to lie there, facedown. This is Satan's one-two-punch sequence. First he tempts us, telling us that sin is really no big deal or that no one will find out. Then, when we give in and fall, he tells us how horrible our sin is and that God cannot accept us. He wants to keep us away from God as long as possible.

If you sin, don't let Satan have this second victory! The moment you are convicted of your sin, run back to God. We do not deserve his forgiveness and love, but he offers it nonetheless through Jesus. Let's take it! The following outline contains simple steps you can take to get right with God.

Steps to Getting Right with God

- Plan time when you can be alone and uninterrupted. (Yes, you can.)
- Read James 4:7–9 and Hebrews 10:19–22.
- Pray: "Lord, I want to be right with you. I am returning to you. I want to be close to you. Thank you for your promise to draw near to those who draw near to you! I humble myself before you and confess my desperate need for you. Please show me what is between us. Show me my sin. Show me what I need to let go of and surrender to you. My only hope to come into your holy presence and receive forgiveness for my sin is the death and resurrection of Jesus Christ!"
- Write down every sin he brings to your mind.
- Ask him again, and wait.
- Write down every sin he brings to your mind.
- Do it again.
- Deal with each sin.
  - Read 1 John 1:1–10.
  - Go through each sin on your list individually. Agree with God that it is sin (confession); determine to obey God in this area (repentance); and ask for and receive God's forgiveness and cleansing by the blood of Christ.
  - Ask God in faith to deliver you from bondage, and take back any territory in your life you have given to the enemy.
  - Mark out each item as you receive forgiveness, unless it involves another person.
  - If your sin has hurt another person, plan to ask for forgiveness (Matt. 6:14–15).
  - After you ask each person for forgiveness, mark it out (even if the person doesn't forgive you).
- Create a specific plan for repentance.
  - What plans will you make to do what God has told you to do?
  - What steps can you take to remove this sin and temptation from your life?
  - To whom will you be accountable?

- Walk in truth, joy, freedom, and fullness of the Spirit!
- Take time to confess your sins and get right *every day.*

As you go through this process, here are some areas of sin to consider:

- Thoughts
- Attitudes
- Speech
- Relationships
    - Against whom have you sinned?
    - Whom do you need to forgive?
- Sins of commission: What are you doing that God does not want you to do?
- Sins of omission: What does God want you to do that you are not doing?
- Self-rule, self-reliance
- Finances
- Work
- Entertainment and media
- Are you in bondage to sin? Are you controlled by fear, lies, negative thoughts, food, or sexual immorality?
- Are all parts of your life surrendered to Jesus?

I also recommend two books that will help you go through an in-depth process for getting right with God. A short and powerful book to lead you through confession and renewal is *Returning to Holiness: A Personal and Churchwide Journey to Revival,* by Dr. Gregory R. Frizzell. Another important resource for a more in-depth understanding of bondage to sin and how to be free is *The Bondage Breaker: Overcoming Negative Thoughts, Irrational Feelings, Habitual Sins,* by Neil T. Anderson.

Giving Him All

In addition to getting rid of the sin in our lives, we also make Jesus Lord by surrendering every area of our lives to him. When we restore our relationship with God through Jesus Christ, we are submitting to his authority in our lives. When he died on the cross to pay for our sins and deliver us from bondage, he purchased us as his own possessions. That means that everything about us belongs to him.

Now my thoughts are his. My words are his. My family (spouse, children, parents, siblings), my home, my possessions, my job and career, my hopes and dreams, my body, my time, my energy, and my money are his. I am "called to belong to Jesus Christ" (Rom. 1:6).

This is our prayer: "Lord, I surrender myself and all I have to you! Please show me areas of my life that I have not surrendered to you as Lord. Show me what you want me to do with my life and all I have. Whatever you want me to do, no matter what it is, that is what I will do. I know that you love me, and I trust that your will for me is good and right."

Your body is his. He created your physical body and has now bought it again as his own. Your body is a dwelling place of the Holy Spirit, so "you are to glorify God with your body" (1 Cor. 6:19). Two of the most wonderful physical gifts God has given us are food and sex. When these are turned into ungodly, selfish endeavors, they become the most powerful bondages in our lives. Run away from these sins of the body! We must follow Paul's example:

But I discipline my body and keep it under control,
lest after preaching to others I myself should be disqualified.
1 Corinthians 9:27

Another way we honor God with our bodies is to stay as healthy as we can. By staying healthy, we can operate at full energy and longevity in fulfilling God's purpose. This means that we stay disciplined in matters of rest, sleep, exercise, and nutrition. The principle of weekly rest, represented by the laws of the Sabbath in the Old Testament, is also an important and often neglected part of our physical and spiritual health.

Your possessions are his. All that we have has been given to us by God, and as we operate under his lordship, we consider ourselves not owners but stewards. We are taking care of that which belongs to God. What we choose to possess and what we choose to do with what we possess are matters of submission to Christ. This, of course, includes our money. How we spend our money is a reflection of our values and priorities and will therefore reflect the lordship of Christ in our lives. Randy Alcorn writes, "If Christ is not Lord over our money and possessions, then he is not our Lord."[2] Giving a portion of our income is one of the most important ways we acknowledge the lordship of Christ with our possessions. (See Appendix A: The Ministry of Giving for an outline of the New Testament teaching on giving.)

Your relationships are his. A believer's relationship with God is to take absolute priority over all other relationships. We also want to make sure that all of our relationships honor God. As we learn to love and minister to others in chapters 9, 10, and 11, we will discover in more detail how to submit our relationships to Christ.

Your vocation is his. We often make the mistake of thinking that only pastors, missionaries, or other vocational ministers have callings. Those are certainly important callings, but every believer is called to honor God and serve others through his or her vocation. This is one of the most important platforms God gives us for ministry. God will direct you and use you in your work. If you find yourself stuck in a particular vocation or trapped in an undesirable job, ask God what he wants you to do. He may teach you how to transform and revive your work for his glory. Or he may free and provide for you to do something you never dreamed of. Do not limit what God can do in your life!

Your recreation is his. Rest and renewal are important parts of life. The real goal of life is to work and accomplish God's mission. The purpose of rest is to renew our energy and focus so that we can get back to work. Our culture has reversed this and has made entertainment and recreation the goal. People work so that they have enough money to enjoy themselves on the weekends. It is what they plan for and look forward to.

There are so many wonderful things to enjoy: outdoor activities, art, music, books, games, drama, fellowship, and so forth. However, each of these can disproportionately become our focus and obsession. The world has turned so many of these into destructive, sinful activities. What are your hobbies, pastimes, and favorite forms of entertainment? We must ask whether these activities are honoring to Christ and if they are serving the purposes of rest and renewal.

Pray through every area of your life specifically, and surrender each one to Jesus. Ask him to show you what he wants you to do with each.

Discussion Questions

- What is the cost of following Jesus?
- What does it mean to follow Jesus?
- What does it mean to "take up your cross"?
- What does Jesus give us when we follow him?
- How do we make Jesus Lord of our lives?
- What is confession and repentance?
- Will you make Jesus Lord of your life?

Big Ideas

- If you are going to follow Jesus, you cannot live for yourself.
- If you are going to follow Jesus, you cannot live for others.
- If you are going to follow Jesus, you must choose the path of redemptive suffering.
- While we are called to give *all* to Jesus, Jesus gives us *more* in return.
- God is eternal and spirit, and this world is temporary and material. God offers us eternal, spiritual life.
- There are two steps we can take to acknowledge the lordship of Jesus in our lives. The first is to remove sin from our lives. The second is to surrender every part of our lives to God in obedience.
- To confess our sin is to agree with God that what we did was wrong. To repent is to resolve to stop doing it.
- All we must do is agree with God about our sin, receive his forgiveness based on the blood of Jesus, and resolve to trust in God's power to obey.

- We must be able to distinguish the loving, restorative conviction of our Father from the destructive accusations of Satan.
- When Jesus died on the cross to pay for our sins and deliver us from bondage, he purchased us as his own possessions. That means that everything about us belongs to him.

For Further Reading

Alcorn, Randy. 2003. *Money, Possessions, and Eternity.* Carol Stream, Illinois: Tyndale House Publishers. (A smaller book with similar material is *Managing God's Money*, by Randy Alcorn.)

Anderson, Neil T. 2000. *The Bondage Breaker: Overcoming Negative Thoughts, Irrational Feelings, Habitual Sins.* Eugene, Oregon: Harvest House Publishers.

Bonhoeffer, Dietrich. 1995. *The Cost of Discipleship.* New York: Touchstone (first published in 1937).

Frizzell, Gregory R. 2000. *Returning to Holiness: A Personal and Churchwide Journey to Revival.* Memphis: The Master Design.

CHAPTER 3

Spending Time with God

LET'S SUPPOSE THAT THE HAPPY young man in chapter 2, recently engaged, chose not to ask for an annual date with another woman. What if instead he had made this request:

"Sweetheart, I am so excited to be your husband! But I need you to understand that I enjoy long-distance relationships. I would really prefer not to live with you. While I do want to marry you, I don't really want to have to talk with you all that much. And I am not much interested in sharing my stuff, my space, or my time with you."

Once again, I do not know of a woman who desires this kind of marriage. We can continue to learn how to love God by observing our hopes and expectations for marriage. An obvious part of any significant relationship is spending time together. This is also true of our relationship with God.

You have said, "Seek my face."
My heart says to you, "Your face, LORD, do I seek."
Psalm 27:8

God asks us to *seek* him. This means that we spend the time and energy necessary to know him. When the Lord says to seek his *face*, he is talking about intimate fellowship. Our faces are one of the most intimate parts of our bodies. There we find the eyes, which are the windows to the soul. It is amazing to think that God desires this kind of closeness with us!

God wants to seek an intimate fellowship with Him.

We know that an intimate relationship requires time together. We can see this in Jesus's close relationship with the Father. The Bible says that Jesus "would withdraw to desolate places and pray" (Luke 5:16).

And rising very early in the morning, while it was still dark,
he departed and went out to a desolate place, and there he prayed.
Mark 1:35

Jesus taught his disciples to do the same.

But when you pray, go into your room and shut the door
and pray to your Father who is in secret.
And your Father who sees in secret will reward you.
Matthew 6:6

As we see in these passages, when we spend time alone with God, we are communicating with him. Communication is one of the most important parts of developing an intimate relationship with someone. We speak to God through prayer, and we listen to God through the Scripture and the Holy Spirit. We will talk more in depth about these aspects of our relationship with God in the next chapters.

Making a Commitment and Being Consistent

Do you believe that your relationship with God is the most important thing in your life? Are you convinced that spending time with him in intimate fellowship is critical for that relationship? If so, let's resolve to spend time with him every day! Gregory Frizzell writes, "Your prayer time should be 'an absolute commitment'…This emphasizes that your prayer time is a major priority that you carefully schedule and guard…Whatever it takes to insure and guard your time with God, you must do it."[3]

Sometimes I hear that people like to spend time with God while washing the dishes, driving to work, playing golf, or hunting. Enjoying fellowship with God during all our activities is wonderful! However, walking with God throughout the day is not the same as stopping our activities to spend time with God. Our friends and family would not appreciate it if the only time we spent with them was while we were doing something else. A strong relationship requires undivided attention and focused communication.

When resolving to spend this kind of time with God, it is best to make specific commitments. Be sure to include details such as when, how often, where, and how long you will meet with him. Be sure to pick a time when you will be alone and uninterrupted. Be specific about what you will do during this time. The most important elements are prayer, Bible study, and Bible memorization.

While spending time with God at any time of the day is valuable, there are several reasons why the morning time has been most helpful to me. Consider these reasons as you select your own time:

- Early morning is when I am able to find time that is quiet and uninterrupted, before the little children get up and work begins.
- Morning is when my mind is clearest.
- I can set my mind on the Lord and establish an eternal perspective before I start the day.

There is no rule for how much time you should spend with God, but it is important to give yourself enough time so that you do not feel rushed. Frizzell warns, "There is simply no shortcut to a dynamic walk with Christ or to the mountain-moving power of the Holy Spirit."[4] As you choose to spend significant time with the Lord, you will come to love and know God more deeply. As your relationship with him develops, you will want to spend even more time with him!

> There is simply no shortcut to a dynamic walk with Christ.

If you are like me, this is probably not the first time you have resolved to spend time with God. There have been times in my life when I have struggled to be consistent or to have meaningful time with God. Let's review some common obstacles to spending time with the Lord and discuss ways to overcome them.

- "I don't have time or can't get alone." Let me respond to this frankly: yes, you can. Here is a fact: we do what we want to do. We make time for what is important to us. It may require changing your sleeping schedule or going out of your way to find a secluded place. I am not saying it will be easy, but it is possible. And it is worth it!
- "I don't really know how to spend time with God." If you will carefully read the next few chapters of this book, you will be well on your way to knowing how to have a fruitful time with the Lord!
- "I can't get up in the morning." As I said before, having a quiet time at any time in the day is better than having no quiet time at all. But if you would like to make your time with God the priority of your day, then try some of these strategies for getting up in the morning:
    - Go to bed earlier. You may have to work hard to change your sleep schedule.
    - Move your alarm clock away from your bed so that you have to get up to turn it off.
    - Share your goals with others so they can pray for you and hold you accountable.
    - Ask someone to help you get up. A family member or friend can get you up or call you as a form of encouragement and accountability.
- "I can't seem to be consistent." Faithfulness is hard. Sometimes we find the motivation to do something just a few times, but then we can't maintain it. The critical need is to do something long enough to create a life habit. We may have to do something for thirty to sixty days before we form a habit. Here are some things you can do to be consistent:
    - *Remember how desperately you need God.* If we believe we desperately need him, we will seek him. The Bible says that without

him we are able to do nothing, but with him we will accomplish God's purposes.

I am the vine; you are the branches.
Whoever abides in me and I in him, he it is that bears much fruit,
for apart from me you can do nothing.
John 15:5

- *Focus all your energy on this one goal.* Not that this is the only thing you will do, but if you decide that this is the most important issue of life and the most important habit to establish, then you will put all of your focus into it. It will be the highest priority. This is a hill to die on!
- *Gain victory over your flesh by faith.* Paul defines "the passions of the flesh" as "the desires of the body and the mind" (Eph. 2:3). We all have sinful desires and have established habits of the body and mind. In Christ we have the power to overcome sin. As we choose to obey each moment by faith, we will establish new habits of mind and body. We will discuss more about gaining victory over sin in chapter 8.
- *Be aware of the spiritual battle.* Satan does not want us to get close to God and experience his full power. With God's power, we can devastate Satan's plans. Don't let his attempts to keep you from God take you by surprise. (See 1 Pet. 5:8–9; Eph. 6:10–11.)
- *Don't give up!* No one does anything perfectly at first. If you fail, get back up and try again.

For the righteous falls seven times and rises again,
but the wicked stumble in times of calamity.
Proverbs 24:16

- "I have tried to spend time with God before, but I can't seem to connect with him or get anything out of it." This is a common experience. Here are some important things to remember as you seek the Lord.

- *Remember that your goal is to spend personal, interactive time with someone who loves you.* It is easy to see this time as a task on your to-do list instead of time with a loved one. It is even possible to pray and read the Bible without meeting God! We do not meet God in order to make ourselves feel better, to be better people, or to give a good answer to an accountability partner. Ruthlessly consider your motives. Why are you really doing this?
- *Become aware of God's presence.* God is always with us, whether we are aware of it or not. When we become aware of the real, spiritual, personal presence of God in the room with us, even within us, we can begin to meet God!
- *Expect God to meet you.* Do you believe these promises?

Draw near to God, and he will draw near to you.
James 4:8a

You will seek me and find me, when you seek me with all your heart.
Jeremiah 29:13

Ask, and it will be given to you; seek, and you will find;
knock, and it will be opened to you.
For everyone who asks receives, and the one who seeks finds,
and to the one who knocks it will be opened.
Matthew 7:7–8

Blessed are those who hunger and thirst for righteousness,
for they shall be satisfied.
Matthew 5:6

- *Submit to God.* There are often blocks in our relationships with God because we are holding something back. God is asking us to give up our sin and surrender all areas of our lives to him. When we know he is speaking to us about something, but we do not respond, then we will not be able to connect with him in prayer (1 Pet. 3:12).

Do not accept your feelings as reality. Our culture has trained us to take our feelings very seriously. We often make the mistake of measuring our faith or closeness to God by how we feel. The most important demonstration and confirmation of faith is action, not feelings. Our feelings will usually follow the lead of the thoughts we choose to think, the words we choose to say, and the actions we choose to take. No matter how you feel, meet with God. Get on your knees, open your mouth, and call on his name. No matter how you feel, sing to him and praise him. No matter how you feel, open your heart to God's Word and let him teach you.

Your Commitment to Spend Time with God

I resolve to spend time with God…

- How often? ______________________________
- When? ______________________________
- Where? ______________________________
- What will I do? ______________________________
____
____
- Why is this important to me? ______________________________
____
- Who will I share this commitment with and ask for accountability?
____

Praying at All Times

Although we set specific time aside to spend with God, we can still enjoy his presence and fellowship all day long! Read these passages about enjoying continual fellowship with God.

Nevertheless, I am continually with you; you hold my right hand.
You guide me with your counsel, and afterward you will receive me to glory.
Psalm 73:23–24

Pray without ceasing. Give thanks in all circumstances.
1 Thessalonians 5:17–18

Praying at all times in the Spirit.
Ephesians 6:18a

Through him then let us continually offer up a sacrifice of praise to God,
that is, the fruit of lips that acknowledge his name.
Hebrews 13:15

I have made the heading of this section "Praying at All Times" because that is one of the ways the Bible describes what I am talking about. The word "prayer" does not only mean talking to God. Prayer can also refer to the fellowship we have with God as we enjoy his presence. We can also use other phrases like "walking with God" and "abiding in Christ."

God is always with us, but we are not always aware of his presence. How can we become aware of his presence all day, especially when we have tasks and conversations that require our concentration? One thing we can do is to immediately return our thoughts to the Lord between these activities that require concentration. At these times we can offer praise, give thanksgiving, seek his wisdom, confess our sins, and make requests. In this way, we can be talking with God about what we are doing, submitting to the leading of his Spirit, and depending on his strength as we go.

In addition to turning our hearts to the Lord in between these activities, we can also learn to develop *attitudes* of worship and prayer, even *while* we are engaging in activities that require our concentration. While we may not be able to engage in focused intercession all the time, we can set our minds and hearts on God and do all that we do as an offering of love and worship to God. Even practical, nonspiritual tasks can become acts of worship! Paul claims the following:

To the pure, all things are pure.
Titus 1:15

Another wonderful way to enjoy God's presence and keep our minds focused on him is through Scripture meditation. This is when we read or recall Scripture and then think and pray over it. You can write Scripture on a card and carry it with you. You can write it on a sticky note and put it where you will see it frequently: your mirror, the side of your computer screen, or in your car. Even better for meditation throughout the day is to develop the habit of memorizing Scripture. I will give you some ideas on how to develop this habit in chapter 4. As you develop these habits and skills, you will learn to use Scripture as a way to keep your heart and mind focused on Christ throughout your day.

Discussion Questions

- How is your relationship with God?
- Do you spend time with God? How often? How much?
- Will you resolve to spend regular time with God?
- What can we do to be more consistent in spending time with God?
- What can we do to connect with God when we are spending time with him?
- How can we enjoy God's presence all day?

Big Ideas

- An obvious part of any significant relationship is to spend time together. This is also true of our relationship with God.
- Set aside a block of time to focus on your relationship with God.
- When you are struggling to be consistent in your time with God:
  - Remember how desperately you need God.
  - Focus all your energy on this one goal.
  - Gain victory over your flesh by faith.
  - Be aware of the spiritual battle.
  - Don't give up!
- When you are struggling to connect with God during your time with him:
  - Remember that your goal is to have a relationship with God.
  - Become aware of God's presence.
  - Expect God to meet you.
  - Submit to God.
  - Do not accept your feelings as reality.
- Although we set time aside to spend with God, we can still enjoy his presence and fellowship all day long!
  - Between activities that require concentration, we can immediately return our thoughts to the Lord, offering praise, being thankful, seeking his wisdom, confessing our sins, or making requests.
  - When we set our minds and hearts on God, we can engage in these activities with *attitudes* of prayer.

For Further Reading

Frizzell, Gregory. 1999. *How to Have a Powerful Prayer Life: The Biblical Path to Holiness and Relationship with God.* Memphis: The Master Design.

CHAPTER 4

Understanding God's Word—Getting Started

—⁓—

THE SUMMER BEFORE DANA AND I were married, I went to Kenya for several months. In preparation for my trip, Dana put together a packet for me. It had my name and hearts drawn on the outside. It also had the scent of her perfume. Inside were many smaller packets and envelopes. Dana made a weekly packet that contained a letter plus a Bible verse or love note for every day! I cherished the time each day when I opened these notes and letters. I smelled the packet and opened the notes with a grin of anticipation on my face. They were full of words of love, affection, and encouragement. Although I could not see her, I felt close to her. I was reassured of her love for me, and my commitment and love for her was renewed.

God has also expressed his love for us through the written word. One of the most awesome and basic qualities of God is that he is a God who communicates with us. He reveals himself to us is many ways. We already discussed in chapter 1 how he has revealed himself through creation. God also speaks personally with his own voice, through messengers (prophets, angels), through dreams and visions, and by his Holy Spirit. He revealed himself perfectly by coming to earth as a man, the Lord Jesus Christ (Heb. 12:1–2)! We will now talk about one of the most important way he has spoken to us—through the Bible.

About the Bible

The Bible is often called God's Word. It is made up of sixty-six smaller books and letters that were written by at least fifty authors over a span of two thousand years! There are thirty-nine books in the Old Testament (or Old Covenant), which contain the history, law, poetry, and prophecies of God's people, the Israelites. There are twenty-seven books in the New Testament (or New Covenant), which contain the history and teaching of Jesus and the early church. The Old Testament was written in Hebrew and the New Testament in Greek. Through his Word God teaches us what the Bible is and why what he has written to us is so important.

- *The Bible contains knowledge that we can only know because God has revealed it* (Rom. 1:2–4; Heb. 1:1–2). We can learn many things about God by observing his creation. But there are some things that he has told us about history, himself, and his plan that we would not know unless he told us about it in the Bible. For example, God has revealed in Scripture important truths about creation, the Gospel, the coming of Christ, and the final judgment.
- *The Bible is inspired by the Holy Spirit* (2 Tim. 3:16; 2 Pet. 1:20–21). Although the books of the Bible were written by human authors, God is the ultimate author. He used human authors to speak to us through the Bible.

For we did not follow cleverly devised myths
when we made known to you the power and coming of our Lord Jesus Christ,
but we were eyewitnesses of his majesty…
No prophecy of Scripture comes from someone's own interpretation.
For no prophecy was ever produced by the will of man,
but men spoke from God as they were carried along by the Holy Spirit.
2 Peter 1:16, 20–21

- *The Bible is trustworthy (inerrant)* (2 Pet. 1:19). Since the Bible was not created by man, but was given by God, we know that it is true.

The law of the LORD is perfect, reviving the soul;
the testimony of the LORD is sure, making wise the simple;
the precepts of the LORD are right, rejoicing the heart;

the commandment of the LORD is pure, enlightening the eyes;
the fear of the LORD is clean, enduring forever;
the rules of the LORD are true, and righteous altogether.
Psalm 19:7–9

- *The Bible is authoritative.* Since the author of the Bible is God and it is a trustworthy presentation of truth and righteousness, then it is authoritative. This means that anything we believe to be true or that others tell us is true should be tested against Scripture. If something we think or hear does not agree with the Bible, then we should adjust it to align with what God says is true. This also means that we are responsible for obeying the directions and instructions God gives us in his Word.
- *The Bible is sufficient.* It is the only source of revelation given or needed to understand the truth about God and his will for us. The Bible reveals the Gospel for salvation and truth to equip believers for righteousness (Ps. 19:7–11; Acts 20:32).

All Scripture is breathed out by God and profitable
for teaching, for reproof, for correction, and for training in righteousness,
that the man of God may be complete, equipped for every good work.
2 Timothy 3:16–17

- *God has given his Spirit to help us understand and apply what he has revealed in Scripture* (1 Cor. 2:6–16; John 16:5–15).

The Bible also teaches us what role it should play in our lives:

- The Bible should be read, preached, and taught in the home and in the church (1 Tim. 4:6, 13; 2 Tim. 2:2, 3:14–17, 4:1; Titus 1:9; Deut. 6:4–7).
- The Bible should be used to establish sound doctrine and practice and to refute wrong doctrine and practice (2 Tim. 3:16, 4:2; Titus 1:9–11).

- The Bible should be read, memorized, and meditated upon as a constant source of wisdom and strength (Col. 3:16; 2 Pet. 1:19; Ps. 19:7–8, 1:1–2, 119:9–16; Josh. 1:8).

Benefits of Knowing and Obeying God's Word

The Bible has a lot to say about what happens when we know and obey God's Word. Here are just a few passages. When we obey God's Word:

- We are blessed (Ps. 1:1–3).
- We are vibrant and fruitful (Ps. 1:1–3).
- We become wise for salvation through faith in Jesus Christ (2 Tim. 3:14–17).
- We become mature, equipped for every good work (2 Tim. 3:14–17).
- We are built up (Acts 28:32).
- We are given the inheritance among the sanctified (Acts 28:32).
- Our souls are revived (Ps. 19:7–11).
- We are made wise (Ps. 19:7–11).
- We have joy in our hearts (Ps. 19:7–11).
- Our eyes are enlightened (Ps. 19:7–11).
- We are warned (Ps. 19:7–11).
- We have great reward for keeping it (Ps. 19:7–11).
- We are kept pure (Ps. 119:9–11).
- We are given power in prayer (John 15:7).

Praying God's Word

The Bible has often been described as a letter from God to his people. One important difference between a letter and the Bible is that we usually write letters to people who are not with us. We figure that if we are with someone, then we don't have to write because we can just say what we want to communicate. But when we read the Bible, we are reading what he has written to us *and* we are with him! The Bible is part of our conversation with God.

As mentioned above, the Spirit of God is present, helping us understand and apply what the Bible teaches.

Praying the Bible is an important concept to understand because we so easily make Bible reading an intellectual exercise. That is, we are only using our brains to figure out what the words are saying. Reading the Bible certainly includes using our brains, but it is much more. If we turn Bible reading into an educational or intellectual exercise only, instead of a personal conversation with God, then we have missed its fundamental purpose. This is what Jesus said to the religious Jews:

You search the Scriptures because you think that in them you have eternal life;
and it is they that bear witness about me,
yet you refuse to come to me that you may have life.
John 5:39–40

So what does it mean to pray the Bible? Praying the Bible means immediately responding to the words and ideas in the Bible through prayer. You will find truths and principles that you can pray for others. You will discover promises to claim through prayer. There are many praises and thanksgivings to God in Scripture that you can immediately offer to him. Talk to God about what you are reading. Be sensitive to the ways that his Spirit is speaking to you through the Scripture, and respond to what he is bringing to your mind. What you read might even trigger a thought that does not seem to be directly related to the passage. You can pray about that, too.

You can learn more about this kind of conversation with God in the book *Praying the Bible*, by Donald S. Whitney. We will discuss more about the important role of the Bible in our prayer lives in chapters 6 and 7.

Reading God's Word

Based on what we have covered so far about the Bible, it makes sense to read it every day. That would be the bare minimum!

Blessed is the man...[whose] delight is in the law of the Lord, and on his law he meditates day and night.
Psalm 1:1–2

Reading God's Word should be a central part of our daily time with him. So how should we approach reading the Bible? Where do we start? Anywhere in the Bible is great! Here are a few ideas and principles to keep in mind.

- *Expose yourself to the entire Bible.* We often gravitate to those portions of Scripture that we find easier to understand or more meaningful to us. However, it is important to understand the epic story of God's relationship to man throughout history and across the Old and New Covenants. It is important to expose ourselves to all the truth principles of Scripture. You can do this by systematically and repeatedly reading through the entire Bible. There are many methods and resources for doing this.
    - You can buy a one- or two-year Bible.
    - You can find a program or application that leads you through the Bible in a certain period of time.
    - You can decide not to put a time limit on it and instead read through the Bible as slowly as you want.
    - Instead of reading straight through, many people like to read different portions of the Scripture each day or week. For example, you might read a passage from the Old Testament, from Psalms and Proverbs, and something from the New Testament. Most one-year programs are designed this way.
- *Read whole books of the Bible.* The best way to understand the meaning of a sentence or verse is to understand how it fits into its larger context (the paragraph, section, and book). So make it a habit to read larger portions of Scripture instead of isolated verses. If you decide to do an in-depth study of a particular book of the Bible, there are some Bible study guidelines in chapter 5 that will help.
- *Ask specific questions.* No matter what you are reading, be sure to make it personal and practical. This is not just a history lesson or

an exploration of ideas. It is a personal encounter with God. It is an opportunity for God to speak to you with encouragement and direction. Here is a list of questions you might use as you read:

1. Summarize the story or teaching in one to three sentences.
2. What can I learn about the character and ways of God from these verses?
3. What examples of obedience or faith do I find in these verses ?
4. Do I have any questions that require further study?
5. How is God speaking to me through this Scripture?
6. What am I going to do in response to his leading?
7. Write or voice a prayer to God in response to what he has shown you.

- *Journal as you read the Bible.* Journaling is a wonderful habit to develop. It helps you to clarify, organize, and record your thoughts and experiences. It increases your awareness and intentionality in life. For these same reasons, it is helpful to journal as you are reading the Bible. You can use questions like those above to guide your journaling.
- *Study a topic.* Sometimes you might want to read the Bible with a particular question or problem in mind. I recently wanted to study about fasting. After doing a search for the words "fast" and "fasting" on esvbible.org, I read each verse that referred to fasting and identified the main principles related to fasting in each passage. I was careful to read the larger context of each verse in order to accurately understand it. Then I put all of these principles together to get an idea of what the Bible teaches about fasting. You can see the results of that study in chapter 7.
- As you do a study like this, remember that some topics will include several words or ideas. For example, a study on prayer might include Matthew 7:7–11, which does not include the word "prayer." However, the word "ask" appears five times. The strategies presented for studying the Bible in the next chapter will help with this process.

Memorizing God's Word

Another important way that we can understand and apply God's Word is to memorize it.

I have hidden Your Word in my heart that I might not sin against You.
Psalm 119:11

When we have God's Word in our hearts, we are able to recall and meditate on it at any time. When Jesus was tempted by Satan, as he was fasting in the wilderness for forty days, he responded by quoting God's Word (Luke 4:1–13). I do not think he pulled some scrolls out of his satchel and asked Satan to wait a moment while he found a passage that addressed each of the temptations. Like most Jewish boys, he had memorized God's Word.

Memorizing Scripture is challenging. It is often challenging because, in our culture, we are not in the habit of memorizing anything. However, the more you memorize (and the earlier you teach your children to memorize), the more accustomed your mind will become to it. Don't quit because it is hard at first; keep training your memory muscle, and it will become stronger.

The challenge of memorizing Scripture is not just memorizing it the first time but also remembering it after that. I have spent much time memorizing large portions of Scripture that I did not review and therefore could not remember months later. To remedy this, I use a Scripture memory review system. Memorizing Scripture and using a review system takes time. But based on all that we have learned about praying at all times and the importance of God's Word, we know that it is worth it! Here is King David's conclusion about the words of the Lord:

More to be desired are they than gold, even much fine gold;
Sweeter also than honey and drippings of the honeycomb.
Moreover, by them is your servant warned;
In keeping them there is great reward!
Psalm 19:10–11

I have provided detailed instructions for memorizing and reviewing Scripture in Appendix B: A Scripture Memory Review System.

Discussion Questions

- What does the Bible teach about itself?
- What role should the Bible play in our lives?
- What does it mean to pray the Bible?
- What are some strategies you can use as you read the Bible?
- What plans will you make to read the Bible regularly?
- Why is Scripture memory important?
- Will you begin a Scripture memory review system?

Big Ideas

- The Bible contains knowledge that we can only know because God has revealed it.
- The Bible is inspired by the Holy Spirit; it is trustworthy, authoritative, and sufficient.
- God has given his Spirit to help us understand and apply what he has revealed in Scripture.
- The Bible should be:
    - Read, preached, and taught in the home and in the church.
    - Used to establish sound doctrine and practice and to refute wrong doctrine and practice.
    - Read, memorized, and meditated upon as a constant source of wisdom and strength.
- Praying the Bible means immediately responding to the words and ideas in the Bible through prayer.
- Here are some strategies you can use when reading the Bible:
    - Expose yourself to the entire Bible.
    - Read whole books of the Bible.

    - Ask specific questions.
    - Journal as you read the Bible. Study a topic.
- An important way that we can understand and apply God's Word is to memorize it.

For Further Reading

Whitney, Donald S. 2015. *Praying the Bible*. Wheaton, Illinois: Crossway.

CHAPTER 5

Understanding God's Word—Digging Deeper

When I was a kid, my mom organized our household chores by writing them on colorful three-by-five index cards. Each card listed a chore, instructions, and a date of completion. When I would come home from school, my chore cards were laid out for me. Even if I arrived and found that my mom was gone, I was still sure to find that the chore cards were there.

Imagine if one day, my mom came home later in the afternoon and asked me if I had completed my chores.

"Yes, ma'am," I'd answer. So she'd take my cards and begin to review my chores. She'd check to see if the living room had been vacuumed.

"Matt, the carpet is not clean in here!"

"Yes it is; I picked up everything off the floor."

"The card says to vacuum the carpet."

"Well, I decided that what that meant was to pick everything up off the floor..."

Of course, I would never have gotten away with such a thing. We both knew that I knew what the word "vacuum" means.

When we get a letter from someone or a list of instructions from a parent, we know that we don't get to decide what it means. It means what the words say. And if there is any confusion, it means what the writer intended for them to mean.

As we read the Bible, we will soon discover that some of it is difficult to understand. When we ask the question, "What does this mean?" we are assuming that there is some inherent meaning in the text. Most of us naturally understand that we don't get to *decide* what a verse or passage means; instead, our job is to *discover* what it means. Paul encouraged Timothy:

Do your best to present yourself to God as one approved, a worker who has no need to be ashamed, rightly handling the word of truth.
2 Timothy 2:15

This verse implies that it is possible to not rightly handle the word of truth. One important way that we can rightly handle the word of truth is by rightly understanding what it means.

As we read the Bible, we are asking, "What did the author of this book mean?" and, more importantly, "What is God saying to us today?" If we assume that the Bible has certain meanings, just like a letter from a person, then we know it is possible to misinterpret it. When we read the Bible, our goal is to discover the truth that God has revealed to us in it. Often, this requires more study than just "reading." So in this chapter, we are going to discuss in more detail how to study the Bible. There are some important skills and tools that will help us properly understand what God is saying to us in his Word.

A Word of Encouragement

Some of the skills and tools suggested in this chapter are not commonly known among Christians. If you are not familiar with them, you may find them challenging to understand and implement. They certainly take some time and energy. However, I would like to encourage you not to give up on it if it seems overwhelming at first.

Even if you don't understand some of these ideas when you first read them, just continue reading through the whole chapter. You can come back later and think through the parts you didn't understand. Don't feel that you have to tackle this all at once, either. You can just select one or two skills to work on at first and then come back later to work on the others.

I also want you to know that I believe you *can* understand and use these tools in your own life. Serious Bible study is not just for pastors and teachers. All Christians can take seriously the responsibility of rightly handling the Scripture.

Finally and most importantly, don't let any difficulty of this chapter prevent you from continuing with this book. Understanding this chapter is not necessary for you to benefit from the rest of the book.

To start off, let's get a bird's-eye view of the process. There are three basic steps to understanding the Bible:

1. *Find out what the author was originally saying to his audience.* This is sometimes called "exegesis."
2. *Identify the truth principles.* A truth principle is something that is always true for all people. This is sometimes broadly called "theology," which means "the study of God."
3. *Identify appropriate ways to apply the truth principles to our lives.* We will refer to this as "application."

Identify the Original Meaning

The first step is to discover what the human author was trying to say to his audience. Sometimes this seems obvious. At other times, we might read something that seems to have several possible meanings. How can we know what the author meant? We can't know for sure what the author was thinking, but we can study the text in a way that takes seriously the meaning of the words, the structure of the sentences and paragraphs, and the historical context of the message. By doing this, we should be able to discover what the author was trying to say.

Study Words

When we are trying to understand the Bible, sometimes we have to do extra work to understanding the meanings of words. This is usually when we come upon a word that seems important to the meaning of the passage or when we are not familiar with it. Sometimes it helps to simply look up the English definitions of a word, but it is often necessary to go deeper. This is when it is important to understand that the Bible was originally written in Hebrew and Greek and that someone has translated it into English for us. There are helpful resources available that tell us the various possible meanings of the words in the original language. For example, *Mounce's Complete Expository Dictionary of Old and New Testament Words* (*MED*), by William D. Mounce, is an excellent resource. Mounce also includes a helpful section called "How to Do Word Studies."[5]

One of the first steps to doing a serious word study is to find out from which Hebrew or Greek word the English word you are investigating is translated. You can use an exhaustive concordance to do this. When you look up a word in an exhaustive concordance, you will find the Hebrew or Greek word from which it is translated and a list of the verses in which the word appears. There are several exhaustive concordances available based on different English translations. You can also use an interlinear Bible or Bible-study software to identify the original words. An interlinear Bible lines up the English translation with the original words from which they are translated.

For example, if we are studying 2 Timothy 3:16, we may want to take a closer look at the words *teaching*, *reproof*, *correction*, and *training*. Using a concordance, you will be able to discover the Greek words from which these words have been translated. As we study these verses, we should ask how these terms are different and how they relate to each other. You can see an example of how to use these tools to study words in Appendix C: Word Studies from 2 Timothy 3:16.

As you look up the meanings of words, you will notice that most words have several meanings. It is important to remember that unless someone is making an intentional play on words (like a pun), then a word has only one meaning when it is used in a sentence. How can you tell which of a word's possible meanings is the one intended in the verse you are studying? The answer is this: you can tell by the context. When you read the rest of the sentence and paragraph—and even the rest of the book—you will be able to tell which meaning is intended. This is why it is helpful to study the structure of sentences and paragraphs.

Study the Structure of Sentences and Paragraphs

When I talk about the structure of a sentence, I am referring to the how words in a sentence relate to each other. The basic structure of a sentence starts with a subject and a verb. They relate to each other because the verb tells what the subject is doing. Most of the other words in the sentence are simply telling us more about the subject or the verb.

Looking at sentence structure is especially helpful when studying teaching material in the Bible, such as when Jesus is preaching in the Gospels or when Paul is giving instructions in one of his letters. One helpful tool for discovering the structure of a passage is called a *structural diagram*. Here is an example of one:

"Oh no, I am having grammar class flashbacks!" I know, but take a deep breath and let me encourage you to press on. I can honestly say that for me, learning to do structural diagrams has been one of the most helpful tools for understanding God's Word. Let me explain just two aspects of grammar that are helpful for finding the structure of a passage:

- An *independent clause* is the part of a sentence that makes sense by itself. It is also called a *complete sentence*, which has a subject and a verb. In 2 Timothy 3:14, the first independent clause is "continue in what you have learned." The subject is implied ("you"), and the verb is "continue." Paul is telling Timothy to do something, so we call the verb an imperative (command): "*You* continue in what you have learned." This part of the sentence can stand alone.
- A *dependent clause* is the part of a sentence that tells us more about the independent clause. You can recognize it because it does not make sense by itself. In 2 Timothy 3:14, the clause "knowing from whom you learned it" does not make sense by itself. In the diagram, "knowing" is centered under the verb "continue," because that is what it modifies. Paul is saying that knowing (or remembering) from whom he learned what he believes will help Timothy continue in these beliefs.

2 Timothy 3:14-17
But as for you,
continue in what you have learned
and
have firmly believed,
knowing from whom you learned it
and
how from childhood you have been acquainted
with the sacred writings,
which are able to make you wise
for salvation
through faith.

All Scripture is breathed out by God
and
profitable for teaching,
for reproof,
for correction,
and
for training in righteousness,
that the man of God may be complete
equipped for every good work.

Here are some guidelines for creating a structural diagram:

- Place independent clauses all the way to the left margin.
- Center the first word of a dependent clause (or modifying phrase) below the word it modifies. If the dependent clause or modifying phrase comes before the word it modifies in the order of the text, then center the first word of the clause or phrase *above* the word it modifies.
- Connecting words (*and*, *but*, *then*, *therefore*, and so forth) go on lines by themselves. Line the connectives up with the words they are connecting. (See diagram.)
- Line up parallel ideas, as in this example:

  profitable for teaching,
  for reproof, for correction,
  and
  for training in righteousness

Diagrams like this work much better when using translations of the Bible that follow the grammatical structure of the original language, such as the New King James Version, English Standard Version, and New American Standard Version. You can learn more about structural diagramming in Wayne McDill's book, *12 Essential Skills for Great Preaching.* This book is helpful not just for preachers but for anyone who wants to understand and communicate what the Bible teaches.

Write Down Observations and Questions

As you carefully read and diagram the text, you will begin to notice significant details. You will also come up with questions. Make notes on your observations and questions as you study. Here are some of the observations and questions I had from 2 Timothy 3:14–17.

- Verse 14
  - "But" designates a contrast.

    - With whom is Paul contrasting his reader?
    - Who is the reader?
    - What has he learned and firmly believed?
    - How would he continue in it?
    - From whom did he learn it?
- Verse 15
    - The reader has been acquainted with the sacred writings since childhood.
    - With what sacred writings did he grow up?
    - The sacred writings are able to make one wise for salvation.
    - Salvation comes through faith in Jesus Christ.
- Verse 16
    - What does it mean that the Scripture is "breathed out" by God?
    - What is the difference between teaching, reproof, correction, and training?
- Verse 17
    - How can a person be "complete"?
    - How does Scripture equip someone for good works?
    - For what good works does Scripture equip someone?

There are probably many others. More observations will be made, and many questions will be answered as we continue through the steps of studying Scripture.

Study the Structure of a Book

Just as words relate to each other in a sentence, sentences relate to each other in a paragraph. So also do paragraphs relate to each other to form larger sections, and larger sections work together to convey the overall meaning of a book. Most of the time, our English Bibles do a good job of organizing the paragraph and section breaks.

Follow these steps to discover the overall flow and meaning of a book of the Bible:

- Summarize each paragraph in one sentence.
- Consider how these paragraph summaries relate to each other. You will see that some are closely related and should be grouped together into sections.
- Summarize these larger sections in one sentence.
- As you consider how these summaries of the larger sections relate to each other, you will be able to summarize the entire book in just a few sentences.

As we look at the context of 2 Timothy 3:14–17, we discover that these verses are part of a larger paragraph that probably starts at verse 10. If so, we want to extend our study to include the whole paragraph. As we do, we already get answers to some of our questions.

- Q: With whom is Paul contrasting his reader?
  A: "Evil people and impostors" (v. 13).
- Q: What has he learned and firmly believed?
  A: The writer's teaching, conduct, aim of life, faith, patience, love, steadfastness, persecutions, and sufferings (vv. 10–11).
- Q: How would he continue in it?
  A: To live the same way as the writer (vv. 10–11).
- Q: From whom did he learn it?
  A: The writer of this letter (v. 10).

Next, as we read the whole letter, we learn that the writer is the apostle Paul and that he is writing to Timothy, to whom he refers as "my beloved child" (1:1–2). We also learn that sincere faith dwelt in Timothy's grandmother and mother (1:5). This must be how he was acquainted with the sacred writings since childhood.

You may find it helpful to outline the structure of 2 Timothy as described above. Try it! Don't pass it up because it seems hard or overwhelming. You will be surprised at your ability to do it and what you discover. Once you discern the overall flow and message of the letter, you can identify how the passage you are studying fits into it. Make notes of your discoveries.

Study the History of a Book

When trying to discover what the author was saying to his audience, it is helpful to know more about the author and audience. Why is he writing this book or letter? What is the audience like, and why is this book important to them? What kind of writing is this (letter, history, prophecy, or an apocalyptic [end times] document)?

Many of these questions are answered by reading the entire book. You can also find more information by reading other sources. Study Bibles and Bible commentaries often have good summaries of these details for each book in the Bible. There are also books that introduce the Bible or the Old or New Testaments separately. One example is the *Illustrated Bible Survey: An Introduction*, by Ed Hindson and Elmer Towns. As you read these, however, keep in mind that these books are not Scripture and must continually be tested by Scripture.

Summarize the Message

After you have learned as much as you can about the words, structure, context, and history of a passage, you should be able to accurately identify its primary meaning. As concisely as possible, answer this question: What is the author trying to say to his audience? Once this question can be answered, you are ready to move on to the next part of understanding God's Word.

Identify the Truth Principles

The Bible was not written just for the nation of Israel, Jesus's disciples, or the churches in Corinth, Ephesus, or Rome. It was given for all God's people, for all time. Twice Paul talks about the Old Testament Scriptures in this way:

> *For whatever was written in former days was written for our instruction, that through endurance and through the encouragement of the Scriptures we might have hope.*
>
> Romans 15:4

Now these things happened to them [the Israelites] as an example,
but they were written down for our instruction, on whom the end of the ages has come.
1 Corinthians 10:11

When we discover truth in the Bible that is always true for all people, we have found a *truth principle*. How can we identify these truth principles? This task is often simple. For example, the truth claims in 2 Timothy 3:16–17 are already stated in a clear, universally applicable way. Other passages are more challenging because the truth principles must be extracted from a story or a specific cultural context.

After we identify the message of the author to the original audience, we can ask, "What truth principles does this passage teach?" For example, what do we learn about God, his will, and his ways? What do we learn about God's creation and humanity? What do we learn about what is right and wrong?

You may find many truths in a passage, but each passage has a specific emphasis. You can get at the heart of a passage by following these steps:

1. Identify in one word the theological subject of the passage. This should not be a historical figure. It should be a theological idea, like love, truth, sin, creation, teaching, repentance, prayer, and so forth. This is usually best identified by observing what words and ideas are repeated most throughout the passage.
2. Identify another word that tells more about the main subject. For example, if the passage is about *prayer*, the modifier might be *persistence* or *faith* (thus, persistence in prayer or praying in faith).
3. Identify what this passage teaches about that subject and modifier.

When I was teaching a series on Genesis 15, which tells the story of how God promised to make Abraham's descendants innumerable and to give him the land of Canaan as an inheritance, I concluded that the main theological idea is *promises*. The other prominent theological idea is *trust*. In the story, Abraham is struggling to trust God to fulfill his promises.

I discovered these truth principles from this story:

1. We can trust God for his promise to give us a heavenly home with him.
2. We can trust God for his promises, even when it doesn't look like they can be fulfilled.
3. We can trust God for his promises because he has spoken his Word.
4. We can trust God for his promises and therefore be accepted as righteous by God.
5. We can trust God for his promises, even when the way is difficult (and it will be).
6. We can trust God for his promises as he works out his perfect timing.
7. We can trust God for his promises because he has made a covenant with us.

Being able to identify truth principles in Scripture is a skill that you develop with practice. You might be wondering how I was able to find such specific principles for Christians today from a story about Abraham. I will explain how in the next section on comparing Scripture with Scripture.

Compare Scripture with Scripture

The Bible is made up of many books, but in another sense, it is a single book because it has one author. When we understand that the Bible is one book with God as the author, then we can have confidence that the truth revealed in Scripture will be consistent. This is one of the amazing aspects of Scripture that demonstrates that it is from God. How is it that so many authors and so many books present a coherent view of the world and God?

One way that we will be able to better understand the truth principles of a passage is to see how the passage relates to other parts of the Bible. A study Bible or commentary will list many of the passages in the Bible that relate to the verses you are studying (these are called *cross-references*). Since we know that scriptural truth will be consistent, if what we believe a passage means seems inconsistent with another part of Scripture, we must work to understand how they fit together or how we have misunderstood the meaning.

Here is a classic example of how passages that appear to be in tension work together to give a full picture. Ephesians 2:8–9 teaches that we receive salvation by faith alone and not by works; James 2:14–26 teaches that there is no salvation without works. Upon reflection and further study, we understand that we are saved by faith, not works, and that true faith always produces works.

Another important aspect of comparing Scripture with Scripture is to understand the fulfillment of the Old Covenant in the New Covenant.

> *For since the law has but a shadow of the good things to come*
> *instead of the true form of these realities, it can never,*
> *by the same sacrifices that are continually offered every year,*
> *make perfect those who draw near.*
> Hebrews 10:1

As I studied Genesis 15, I discovered how important this story is in the New Testament and how directly it applies to believers today! God's promise to make Abraham's descendants as numerous as the stars and give the land to them is discussed extensively in Romans 4, Galatians 3, and Hebrews 11:8–16. We learn from these passages that believers in Jesus Christ are the true descendants of Abraham! We are the fulfillment of the promise. We learn that the ultimate fulfillment of the promised land is the heavenly Jerusalem, the city of the living God, which will come from heaven when God establishes the new heavens and the new earth at the end of the age (Rev. 21–22:5)! It was because of these New Testament teachings that I was able to come to the conclusion that God's promises to Abraham were also promises to us.

Apply Truth to Your Life

As we study Scripture, it is important to remember that we are working to understand the Word of our loving Creator and Savior. He is speaking to us!

We are under his authority and gladly submit to the wisdom and goodness of his revelation. Knowledge of God without faith manifested through submission and obedience is useless. So at this point in the process, we are asking the question, "How will I respond in obedience to what God has shown me?"

As we answer this question, it is important to discern the difference between biblical principle and application. *Principles* are always true for everyone, while *applications* are the specific steps of obedience individuals take in different places, at different times. One form of legalism is when a person elevates his or her particular form of obedience to the level of principle or law and expects others to conform to it.

For example, we may look at one of the principles from Genesis 15: "We can trust God for his promises because he has spoken his Word." We acknowledge what a powerful role the Word of God plays in helping us to understand, remember, and hope in God's promises. From this, we can conclude that it is critical to make God's Word an important part of our lives. I might believe that I must obey God in this way by getting up each morning at six o'clock and spending one hour in God's Word reading, praying, studying, and memorizing. This is a good application. However, I must not conclude that every believer must get up at six and spend one hour in Scripture. Others will come to their own specific conclusions about how to respond to this principle.

As you try to understand how to respond in obedience to God's Word, be sure to ask God to lead you in how he wants you to apply his truth. Once you have concluded how best to obey the truth of God's Word in your particular circumstance, the most important thing is to *do it.* A person who understands God's Word but does not respond in obedience is in danger of self-deception and of missing God's blessing! Listen to this warning from James:

But be doers of the word, and not hearers only, deceiving yourselves…
But the one who looks into the perfect law, the law of liberty, and perseveres,
being no hearer who forgets but a doer who acts, he will be blessed in his doing.
James 1:22, 25

Discussion Questions

- What are the three basic steps for understanding the Bible?
- What are some ways we can understand what the author was saying to his audience?
- Are you intimidated by word studies and structural diagrams? Are you willing to try anyway?
- Why is it important to compare Scripture with Scripture?
- What is the difference between biblical principle and application?

Big Ideas

- There are three basic steps to understanding the Bible:
    - Find out what the author was originally saying to his audience.
    - Identify the truth principles.
    - Identify appropriate ways to apply the truth principles to our lives.
- To find out what the author was originally saying to his audience, you can:
    - Study words.
    - Study the structure of sentences and paragraphs.
    - Write down observations and questions.
    - Study the structure of a book
    - Study the history of a book.
    - Summarize the message.
- To identify truth principles from a passage, you can:
    - Identify in one word the theological subject of the passage.
    - Identify a word that tells more about the main subject.
    - Identify what this passage teaches about that subject and modifier.
- As you identify truth principles from a passage, it is important to compare Scripture with Scripture.

- Knowledge of God without faith manifested through submission and obedience is useless.
- It is important to discern the difference between biblical principle and application.

For Further Reading

Hindson, Ed and Elmer L. 2013. Towns. *Illustrated Bible Survey: An Introduction*. Nashville: B&H Publishing Group.

McDill, Wayne. 2006. *12 Essential Skills for Great Preaching*, 2nd ed. Nashville: B&H Publishing Group.

Mounce, William D. 2006. *Mounce's Complete Expository Dictionary of Old and New Testament Words*. Grand Rapids: Zondervan.

CHAPTER 6

Learning to Pray—Biblical Foundations

THE MARRIAGE COUNSELOR TURNED TO Gary and asked, "How is your marriage going? Rate it on a scale between one and ten."

"Well, it isn't perfect, of course," he responded. "But it's not the worst. I guess I'd give it about a seven or eight."

Gary should have seen it coming, but he didn't. His heart sank as the counselor shifted his gaze to his wife. *How will she answer the question?* he wondered.

To his surprise, the counselor turned back to Gary and asked, "How do you think your wife will answer that question?"

Oh, this is even worse, Gary thought. *I have to guess what she would say. Now I'm in double trouble!*

After Gary stumbled through an answer, acknowledging that she would rate the marriage lower on the scale than he did, the counselor said to Gary, "Tell me about the quantity and quality of time you spend together."

Gary continued to squirm in his chair and looked at his watch. *When will this be over?*

How Is Your Relationship with God?

Now, I would like to ask you—how is your relationship with God? As you answer this question, you may think about how close to God you have been in the past. You may also be tempted to compare how close you feel to God with how close to God others appear to be. What if you could ask God to rate how close you are to him? What do you imagine he would say? Here is another question that I believe will help you discover how close you are to God: How is your prayer life?

Most Christians know what it means to pray. We generally believe that it is real and important, but ultimately, many of us feel that we don't really get it, or we have difficulty making prayer a vibrant part of our lives. If we are honest, many of us would admit that prayer is often a dry, unsatisfying experience. We sometimes feel we are not really getting anywhere with it. We struggle with focus and patience and have a hard time being still long enough to have good prayer times.

But there is good news: you can have a dynamic and powerful prayer life! You can have a prayer life in which you enjoy deep intimacy with Christ and see mighty answers to prayer that bring glory to God! Wouldn't you like to be able to read this verse and experience it for yourself?

> *And this is the confidence that we have toward him,*
> *that if we ask anything according to his will he hears us.*
> *And if we know that he hears us in whatever we ask,*
> *we know that we have the requests that we have asked of him.*
> 1 John 5:14–15

As we discussed in chapter 3, prayer is fundamental to our relationship with God. Prayer is a part of our daily time with God as well as our strategy for walking with him throughout the day. In this chapter and the next, we will explore powerful biblical truths about prayer and how to practically incorporate it into our lives.

What Is Prayer?

First, let's back up just a bit and describe what prayer is. Many of us would describe prayer simply as talking to God. This is true, but it is much more. All the ways that we relate to God are a part of prayer. Prayer includes worshipping God through music and singing, enjoying his love and presence in silence, and listening to him speak to us by his Spirit. Prayer is rejoicing, weeping, waiting, bowing before him, resting in him, and surrendering our hearts to him. As we broaden our understanding of prayer, it is easier to understand how we can "pray without ceasing" (1 Thess. 5:17).

Dr. Gregory Frizzell describes prayer in this way: "From God's perspective, prayer is the expression of that which He desires most—your personal relationship of love, surrender and trust. Prayer must be viewed as your commitment to spend meaningful time in personal relationship with God."[6]

Who Prays?

Have you ever read the biographies of mighty Christian heroes? So often, one of the primary aspects of their lives is powerful prayer. It may be tempting for us to conclude, "Well, of course, pastors and missionaries must pray that way." I believe it is common for us to imagine that there is a category of people labeled "spiritually mature," and that we are not in that category and probably never will be. We assume that we are just the common people, the average Christians. Let's test that assumption with these questions: Whom does God love? With whom does he want to have an intimate relationship?

> You will not begin to pray when you become spiritually mature, you will become spiritually mature when you begin to pray.

God loves you! God loves all of us. He has created *each one* of us with the capacity and need to live in deep fellowship with him. Anyone can enter into intimate fellowship with Christ and enjoy a powerful life of prayer. The invitation to know Christ fully and enjoy his perfect love is open to all!

Another common mistake people make is to put off pursing serious prayer lives because they figure that someday, they will grow into maturity and then will be more serious about prayer. Unfortunately, this thinking is backward. Do you want to be spiritually mature? Pray. You will not begin to pray when you become spiritually mature; you will become spiritually mature when you begin to pray.

Why Is Prayer Important?

In order to build a strong foundation for a life of prayer, we have to understand its vital role in the Christian's life. Here are six reasons that prayer is important:

- Prayer is important because relating to God is important. That's what prayer is—relating to God. Relating to God is our very purpose for existence!
- Prayer is important because through prayer, we find life and peace.

For everyone who calls on the name of the Lord will be saved.
Romans 10:13

Do not be anxious about anything,
but in everything by prayer and supplication with thanksgiving
let your requests be made known to God.
And the peace of God, which surpasses all understanding,
will guard your hearts and your minds in Christ Jesus.
Philippians 4:6–7

- Prayer is important because our relationship with God is evidence of our saving faith.

And without faith it is impossible to please him,
for whoever would draw near to God must believe that he exists
and that he rewards those who seek him.
Hebrews 11:6

- Prayer is important because God will lead and help us when we call on him (Heb. 13:20–21).

Let us then with confidence draw near to the throne of grace,
that we may receive mercy and find grace to help in time of need.
Hebrews 4:16

- Prayer is important because God will accomplish his will on earth through prayer (Matt. 6:10). It is often hard to believe, but prayer actually changes things. The author of Hebrews believed that prayer would help him to be restored to them sooner (Heb. 13:18–19). We cannot assume that God's will and provision will be accomplished whether or not we pray.

You do not have, because you do not ask.
James 4:2b

- Prayer is a critical part of the spiritual battle (Eph. 6:17–18).

Put on the whole armor of God,
that you may be able to stand against the schemes of the devil…
praying at all times in the Spirit, with all prayer and supplication.
To that end keep alert with all perseverance, making supplication for all the saints.
Ephesians 6:11, 18

How Do We Pray?

I have often wondered, *How does prayer work?* I could ask a similar question about how to use a car or a computer. We want to know how to drive so we can get to where we are going or what buttons to push to get the outcomes we desire. We want to know how to pray correctly so that we can have our prayers answered. Maybe there is a magic word. If I say "In Jesus's name" at the end of my prayers, will they be answered? What are the rules of prayer?

I know a man who did a forty-day fast. As he related his experience to me afterward, he was angry because God didn't do what he expected. He had expected that if he did a forty-day fast, he would certainly get God's attention, and God would answer his prayers. God didn't; so what was he missing?

Many Christians claim to have had their prayers answered, but so many of these are not particularly impressive. Some of us secretly wonder if these are genuine examples of answered prayer or just well-timed coincidences. Then there are the undeniable answers to prayer. Elijah prayed the rain would stop, and it did. He prayed for the rain to return, and it did (1 Kings 17:1, 18:41–46; James 5:17). He also prayed for fire to come down from heaven to consume the sacrifice, and it did (1 Kings 10:20–40)!

Yes, but those are Bible stories, you might be thinking. Okay, what about George Mueller? He was on his way to preach in America when a thick fog forced his ship to stop. Mueller went to the captain and asked what was happening. When the captain explained, Mueller asked the captain to join him in his cabin. They got down on their knees, and Mueller asked God to remove the fog so that he would be able to make his preaching appointment. When the shocked and confused captain left the cabin, he could not believe his eyes. The fog was gone!

Was this just a well-timed coincidence? How can someone pray this way? I don't know about you, but I long to pray with power for God's purpose and glory. I don't want to accept the status of second-rate Christian. Do you believe that God desires to use *you* through powerful prayer?

So how do we have this kind of prayer life? How do we learn to pray? I would like to share with you the secret of powerful prayer. If there are any rules for prayer, I think this is the most important one: *submit to God.*

Submitting to God

This is a long passage. But please read it slowly and carefully.

You do not have, because you do not ask.
You ask and do not receive, because you ask wrongly,
to spend it on your passions. You adulterous people!
Do you not know that friendship with the world is enmity with God?
Therefore whoever wishes to be a friend of the world makes himself an enemy of God.
Or do you suppose it is to no purpose that the Scripture says,
"He yearns jealously over the spirit that he has made to dwell in us"?
But he gives more grace. Therefore it says,
"God opposes the proud, but gives grace to the humble."
Submit yourselves therefore to God. Resist the devil, and he will flee from you.
Draw near to God, and he will draw near to you.

Cleanse your hands, you sinners, and purify your hearts, you double-minded.
Be wretched and mourn and weep.
Let your laughter be turned to mourning and your joy to gloom.
Humble yourselves before the Lord, and he will exalt you.
James 4:2–10

The only way we can come to God is in humility and submission. When we come to God in prayer, we are not trying to tell him what we need or want. When we come to God, we must admit that only he knows what we need and what we want, and only he can give it to us.

We must come and ask, "Lord, what do I need? What do you want to give me?" And he begins, "I want to give you myself. I am all you need." And then you rest. You receive. You accept his love and forgiveness. You stop striving, stop worrying, stop beating yourself up, stop holding onto sin. You just let go of everything and receive his love. You accept it unconditionally for all that it means. You receive his will for whatever it is because you know that he is good.

> "The great secret of prayer is to align ourselves to God's purposes rather than seeking to align Him to ours."

Then you can ask, "What do you want to do in my life? What do you want to do in the lives of the people around me? What do you want to accomplish in the world?" This is when you can begin to intercede. This is submission in prayer.

Jesus promised to answer prayer. But he also added qualifications to this promise. Here are some of those qualifications:

- "Whatever you ask in my name, this I will do, that the Father may be glorified in the Son" (John 14:13).
- "If you abide in me and my words abide in you, ask whatever you wish and it will be done for you" (John 15:7).
- "If we ask anything according to his will…we know that we have the requests that we have asked of him" (1 John 5:14–15).

These are descriptions of submission to God. Submission is letting go of our own agendas, desires, hopes, and fears and instead seeking to know his will and character. There are three important ways we can submit to God in prayer.

1. *Seek to grow closer to God in prayer.*
   The ultimate purpose of prayer is the same as our purpose for life: to love him, to know him, to worship him, and to enjoy his presence and love. If you feel that you don't understand prayer, this is the place to start. Don't try to get answers to prayer; don't try to understand how prayer works. Just pray so that you can know and love him. As these verses affirm, God wants our hearts, not just our words.

This people draw near with their mouth and honor me with their lips,
while their hearts are far from me.
Isaiah 29:13–14

You will seek me and find me,
when you seek me with all your heart.
Jeremiah 29:13

   If this isn't our primary objective in prayer, then we will never be able to understand it.

2. *Pray according to the truth of God's Word.*
   How can we learn the heart of God? How can we know his character, ways, and will? We can know these things because he has revealed them in his Word. The deeper we grow in our understanding of Scripture, the deeper will be our understanding of God, and the better we will know how to pray.

   For example, God reveals in Scripture that our priority and focus should be on the eternal and spiritual.

Do not lay up for yourselves treasures on earth…
but lay up for yourselves treasures in heaven.
Matthew 6:19–20

Seek the things that are above, where Christ is…
Set your minds on things that are above, not on things that are on earth.
Colossians 3:1–2

We should certainly pray for material provision and physical healing. However, the more we have the heart of God, the more we will pray for God's eternal, spiritual purposes to take place in people's lives.

In addition to praying according to the principles we discover in Scripture, we can also pray the prayers we find in Scripture. We can learn how to pray by looking at Paul's prayer requests and the prayers he offers for others (Eph. 1:15–19, 3:14–21, 6:18–20; Col. 1:9–12, 4:2–4). Paul prayed for the Colossians:

And so, from the day we heard, we have not ceased to pray for you,
asking that you may be filled with the knowledge of his will
in all spiritual wisdom and understanding.
Colossians 1:9

3. *Follow the leading of God's Spirit in prayer.*
   As we have seen, prayer is not just talking to God. Prayer includes listening. In addition to his Word, another way that God speaks to us is by his Spirit. Dr. Frizzell explains:

   > Listening to God is the fundamental key to an effective prayer life. All genuine prayer starts with God Himself! After all, prayer is not telling God what He is to do. Prayer is our discovering what God wants to do and joining Him as co-laborers through our prayers. Through meditating, you learn to hear

> God's leading and thus your prayers initiate from His heart and mind.[7]

As you pray, the Holy Spirit will remind you of his Word, character, and will. He will also lead you to pray in specific ways for specific situations. How did Elijah know that God would stop the rain and bring the fire? I don't think these were his own ideas. God told him to ask for these things. He was asking in faith because he knew it was what God wanted. How did George Mueller know that God would remove the fog? I believe that he was in such close fellowship with God, and so sensitive to the leading of his Spirit, that he knew that was what God wanted to do.

How do we know the difference between God's leading and our own random thoughts? Or worse, what if some other spirit is speaking to us? The Bible teaches us how to recognize the voice of God.

- The Spirit speaks, reminds us of, and agrees with the Word of God (Eph. 6:17; John 16:13).
- The Spirit will acknowledge and glorify Jesus (1 John 4:1–4; John 16:14).
- The Spirit brings peace, order, conviction, and righteousness. He does not bring doubt, confusion, guilt, or evil (John 16:8–11; Gal. 5:16–26).

These are the biblical signs of the work of the Holy Spirit. When God speaks to us through his Spirit, he will speak according to his Word, he will glorify Jesus, and he will bring righteousness and peace!

Discussion Questions

- How is your relationship with God?
- How is your prayer life?

- Do you believe you can have a dynamic and powerful prayer life?
- Why is prayer important?
- What is the secret of a powerful prayer life?
- What are three important ways to submit to God in prayer?
- How do we know when God is speaking to us by his Spirit?

Big Ideas

- You can have a dynamic and powerful prayer life!
- Every way that we relate to God is a part of prayer.
- Prayer is the expression of your personal relationship with Christ.
- You will not pray when you become spiritually mature; you will become spiritually mature when you pray.
- There are six reasons that prayer is important:
    - Prayer is important because relating to God is important.
    - Prayer is important because through prayer, we find life and peace.
    - Prayer is important because our relationship with God is evidence of our saving faith.
    - Prayer is important because God will lead and help us when we call on him.
    - Prayer is important because God will accomplish his will on earth through prayer.
    - Prayer is important because it is a critical part of the spiritual battle.
- The only way we can come to God is in humility and submission.
- As Dr. Frizzell writes, "The great secret of prayer is to align ourselves to God's purposes rather than seeking to align Him to ours."
- Here are three important ways to submit to God in prayer:
    - Aim to grow closer to God in prayer.
    - Pray according to the truth of God's Word.
    - Follow the leading of God's Spirit in prayer.

- When God speaks to us through his Spirit, he will speak according to God's Word, he will glorify Jesus, and he will bring righteousness and peace!

CHAPTER 7

Learning to Pray—Biblical Strategies

My first date with Dana was on her birthday. I remember how pretty she looked, her beautiful smile, and her bubbly laugh. I took her to one of the nicest restaurants in the area. We had been friends for a while, but now that we were on a date, we both knew that our relationship was taking a new direction. There was certainly a sense of nervousness and anticipation. Maybe that is why Dana didn't have much to say. I continued to enjoy her beautiful smile and bubbly laugh, but that was about it. There wasn't really much conversation!

We have all probably been in situations in which we were really not sure what to talk about or what to say to someone. Awkward! It is often no different when we meet with God. Many Christians are not sure exactly where to start or what to talk about. But sometimes we also encounter people who never run out of things to say. This is equally frustrating because we don't get to contribute much, or we become unhappy with the direction of the conversation. In the same way, we shouldn't just babble on in prayer. We must be sensitive to how God wants to direct the conversation.

Fortunately, the Bible helps us understand what kinds of things the Lord desires to talk with us about. In general, there are four aspects of prayer: worship, confession, intercession, and personal requests. Let's discuss each one.

Worship

Worship is a great place to start your time with God.

Come into his presence with singing!
Enter his gates with thanksgiving and his courts with praise!
Psalm 100:2b, 4a

You don't have to start here. As you come to God, he may immediately convict you of sin or lead you to pray for someone. But in general, beginning with worship is appropriate and effective. When we praise and give thanks to God, we are reminded of his love, power, and goodness.

Many believers find it difficult to begin with worship. Most people in our culture seem to make decisions based on how they feel. If they don't feel like doing something, they don't do it, even when they know it is right. When they feel like doing something, they do it, even when they know it is wrong. We often do not feel like praying. We don't feel worshipful, thankful, or loving toward God, so we don't do it. Many people seem to operate like they *have* to obey their feelings. However, you do not need to be a slave to your feelings and desires.

You can choose to do the right thing, no matter how you feel or what you want. And amazingly, when you choose by faith to do what is right, your feelings and desires will eventually follow! Therefore, worship is transformative. It will change our attitudes and feelings. So just start praising. Thank God for all the good things in your life. Read Scripture about how awesome he is, and respond in praise. No matter how you feel, begin singing praises to God. Get on your knees. Lift up your hands. *Choose* to worship him.

In my prayer time, I am committed to worshipping until I am changed. I keep pressing in, seeking and praising him, until I have a new perspective. Worship produces a clear view of God, which gives us hope, joy, and peace. Keep worshipping until you get there!

> Prayer is not trying to get somewhere, it is the place you are seeking to be.

Dr. Frizzell reflects, "You cannot praise only when you 'feel' like it. Never forget, the deepest praise and worship is based on a choice, not a feeling. In fact, the deepest worship of your life will be done at times of greatest darkness and pain."[8]

Another important aspect of our time of worship is to make sure that we are not in a hurry. Sometimes we see prayer time as a task on our to-do list, something we need to get done so that we can move on to something else. We may feel rushed because we are trying to get to the next thing. This is not a good mind-set for worship. Prayer, especially worship, is not trying to get somewhere; it is the place you are seeking to be: the presence of God. This is where you stop and rest. There is no hurry in eternity. Be quiet and still, and enjoy God's presence.

One of my favorite ways to worship is through music. Music is powerful! It can help us focus on and draw near to God. You can sing to God, play your instruments for him, or listen to worship music. I have created several playlists of my favorite worship songs. I often let these songs lead me into worship during my time with God.

Confession

We have already discussed confession and repentance of sin in chapter 2. Sometimes it is necessary for us to take an extended period of time to get right with God, but this is usually because we have not given proper attention to our relationship with him. It is much better to make confession a regular part of our daily time with him.

In fact, we can even do better than that! My Sunday School teacher used to tell us that a good barometer of how close we are to God is how long it takes us to confess and return to him after we have sinned. At this point in my life, when I become aware of my sin, I cannot possibly wait until the next morning to get right with God; I have become so addicted to the peace of God that I want to run back to him as soon as possible.

Another reason it is so important to confess our sins is that the Bible teaches that sin becomes a block to our prayers.

If I had cherished iniquity in my heart,
the Lord would not have listened.
Psalm 66:18

Peter also quoted from the Psalms:

For the eyes of the Lord are on the righteous,
and his ears are open to their prayer.
But the face of the Lord is against those who do evil.
1 Peter 3:12

The Bible also teaches that "the prayer of a righteous person has great power as it is working" (James 5:16).

As with other parts of prayer, we cannot be in a hurry when getting right with God. So take the time each day for confession of sin. You may find it helpful to go back to chapter 2 and use the ideas and tools there to guide your times of confession. You can begin with this prayer from the Psalms:

Search me, O God, and know my heart!
Try me and know my thoughts!
And see if there be any grievous way in me,
and lead me in the way everlasting!
Psalm 139:23–24

Intercession for Others

The Bible teaches that an important part of prayer is intercession for others. To *intercede* means to ask or act on behalf of another. Christians are taught to pray for:

- Brothers and sisters in Christ (Eph. 6:18)
- Lost people (Rom. 10:1; 1 Tim. 2:1–4)
- People in authority (1 Tim. 2:2)

There are many wonderful prayers in the Bible that can help us pray for others. In the book of Ephesians, there are at least three powerful prayers we can offer for others (Eph. 1:15–19, 3:15–21, 6:19–20). Here is one of them:

That according to the riches of his glory he may grant you
to be strengthened with power through his Spirit in your inner being,
so that Christ may dwell in your hearts through faith—
that you, being rooted and grounded in love,
may have strength to comprehend with all the saints
what is the breadth and length and height and depth,
and to know the love of Christ that surpasses knowledge,
that you may be filled with all the fullness of God.
Ephesians 3:16–19

As you pray for others, you may find it helpful to keep a list of the people and needs you are praying for. There are many ways to do this, so find a tool or method that helps you consistently pray for others.

Personal Requests

The Bible also teaches us to bring our personal requests to God (Phil. 4:6). We can talk to God about anything and everything in our lives. We can seek to know his will and direction for any question or decision pertaining to life. We can talk to God about our physical health, spiritual growth and character, relationships, work, and material needs. All the other principles in this chapter and the last play important roles in what types of requests we make concerning these matters. In the next section (on focus), we will discuss more about making personal requests.

We can talk to God about anything and everything in our lives.

—~—

Now that we have discussed the four types of prayer, we will cover how to pray with focus, faith, and fasting.

Pray with Focus

Many people tell me that their greatest challenge in prayer is staying focused. I can relate. Sometimes I feel like my mind has a mind of its own! It goes wherever it wants; it chases after every distracting thought. Here are some effective strategies for staying focused while you pray.

Pray the Bible

Check out the section on praying the Bible in chapter 4. Praying the Bible has been one of the most helpful ways for me to stay focused. We are not just reading or thinking; we are having a real conversation with God!

Pray Out Loud

Often, in Scripture, prayer is described as lifting one's voice to the Lord. But it is common today for us to pray silently. When I pray silently, it seems like my prayers just bounce around in my head with the rest of my distracting thoughts. When I pray out loud, it forces me to choose my words and use my mouth, and then I also hear the prayer I am offering. This brings an amazing intentionality and focus to my prayers.

When I am struggling to focus my thoughts or get my heart in the right place, the quickest way of cutting through the distraction and wrong attitudes is to physically lift up my voice to God. I find it freeing and empowering. It gives me real traction in starting my time with the Lord.

Use Prayer Postures

In addition to lifting one's voice, there are many references in Scripture to the positions people assume during prayer. Some pray standing and some kneeling. Some lie down on their faces, bow, or lift their hands to the Lord. I find that taking such positions in prayer helps me to stay focused on what I am doing. It also helps me to develop a more humble and worshipful attitude toward the Lord. Can you pray in a normal, sitting position? Of course! You can pray in any position. But for me, praying silently while sitting in a chair is the recipe for a nap!

Pray about Whatever Is on Your Mind

Have you ever gone to church and heard one of the worship leaders say, "Leave your troubles at the door, and come in and worship the Lord!" Leave our troubles at the door? Is this the picture of prayer we see in the Bible? No. One of the most important parts of prayer is to *bring* our troubles to the Lord!

One of the reasons we have a hard time staying focused in prayer is because we have a flood of troubles and worries that are demanding our attention. For some reason, we try to hold off those thoughts so that we can focus on prayer. But these are the very worries that God wants us to bring to him!

Casting all your anxieties on him, because he cares for you.
1 Peter 5:7

When your mind is oppressed with issues other than those on your prayer list, don't worry about your prayer list; just pray about what is on your heart. Turn your thoughts over to your Father just as fast as they come to you. Tell him about your troubles; tell him how you feel. Tell him what you want, and ask him what he wants for you. Ask him for wisdom, direction, and strength. Pray for the people who come to mind. Don't worry about keeping things in order or finishing a particular topic. Just pray whatever is on your mind.

Paul explains that we should bring to the Lord those concerns in our lives that could cause anxiety.

Do not be anxious about anything,
but in everything by prayer and supplication with thanksgiving
let your requests be made known to God.
And the peace of God, which surpasses all understanding,
will guard your hearts and your minds in Christ Jesus.
Philippians 4:6–7

Carefully consider all the parts of this verse. We often begin prayer with anxiety. But we can conclude with peace! How does this happen? First, we pray with thanksgiving. Paul encourages us to thank God in all circumstances, not just the good ones (1 Thess. 5:18). James claims that we can even rejoice in our trials (James 1:2)! Second, we make our requests to God about our concerns. Then we encounter an amazing point of faith: trust God with it.

This verse does not say that we are going to have peace after he gives us the answers or after he fixes all our problems. The peace comes simply because we have trusted the matter into the hands of our loving Father. It is important that this peace transcends understanding, because our tendency is to figure things out in our minds. This is usually what we call "worry." We will not have peace because we have figured out a solution but because we have entrusted it to the one who can.

We will not have peace because we have figured out a solution, but because we have entrusted it to the one who can.

Make a To-Do List

Another way that I become distracted during prayer is when the tasks of the day come flooding into my mind. It is tempting to make plans or work out problems I am facing. I often think of things I must do that are not yet on my to-do list. I try to hold these thoughts in the background of my mind while I pray so I won't forget them. These thoughts often distract me from focusing on God in prayer.

I have solved this problem by making sure that I have something to write on when I pray. When I think of an errand to run, a call to make, or a project to work on, I just write it down. Sometimes that's all it takes to get it off my mind, but at other times, I just want to keep thinking about it. This is when I go back to the last strategy: pray about whatever is on your mind. What a great time to ask for God's wisdom and strength for your projects and responsibilities!

Practice Stillness, Quietness, and Focus

Another challenge we face in prayer is that most of us have a difficult time just sitting still. Our culture has trained us to always be watching, reading, saying, doing, or listening to something. We have developed quite short attention spans!

Just because we find that something is hard to do doesn't mean that we can't learn to do it. That's what we call *practice.* The more you try to do something, the smarter, stronger, and more efficient you will be at it. You can even practice being still, quiet, and focused. Take a few minutes each day to make yourself sit still in one position and be quiet. It may take all your mental and physical energy to do this. Remove every possible stimulus you can. Close your eyes.

Once you are still, try to become aware of what is in your mind. At first, you may just be an observer, watching what is going on there. Sometimes this is interesting, and sometimes it is disturbing! But you don't have to observe only; you can direct your mind. After all, it is *your* mind! Try to think of a particular thing, and focus on it. Preferably select a word or verse or attribute of God. Keep practicing, and extend your time. You will find this valuable for your overall strength of mind, self-control, focus, and peacefulness.

Take a Walk

One does not have to be still in order to pray. In fact, another effective strategy for staying focused while you pray is to get out and walk. Surrounding yourself with his creation has a wonderful effect on bringing you closer to the Lord. Some people find that the rhythm and movement of walking also helps free their minds to focus.

Pray in Faith

In addition to praying with focus, we can also learn to pray in faith. Jesus taught his disciples the importance of faith in prayer:

> *And Jesus answered them, "Have faith in God.*
> *Truly, I say to you, whoever says to this mountain,*

'Be taken up and thrown into the sea,'
and does not doubt in his heart,
but believes that what he says will come to pass,
it will be done for him.
Therefore I tell you, whatever you ask in prayer,
believe that you have received it, and it will be yours."
Mark 11:22–24

The author of Hebrews writes:

And without faith it is impossible to please him,
for whoever would draw near to God must believe that he exists
and that he rewards those who seek him.
Hebrews 11:6

We can approach God in prayer with faith because, as Jesus taught in Matthew 7:7–11, God has invited us to pray (v. 7)! He has also promised to answer (v. 8), and he desires to give us good things (vv. 9–11). As we have already seen in 1 John 5:14–15, the key to having confidence that God will hear and answer specific prayers is that we are asking according to his will.

How do we know we are asking something according to his will? This is what we have been talking about all along. We lay aside our own agendas and seek his. We seek an intimate relationship with him. We listen to the leading of his Spirit. We seek his will in his Word. For example, when we read a prayer of Paul for the Ephesians, we can see God's will and desire for us. We can pray this prayer for ourselves and others with confidence. We know this is what God wants to do!

As you learn to pray in faith, don't forget that man's free will is a part of God's will. For example, we cannot pray in faith that someone will be saved, because God's will is for that person to exercise his or her own faith. However, we know that God desires for everyone to be saved, so we can pray with confidence that God will work by his Spirit to bring love and truth into that person's life. We can pray in faith that God will speak to the person and draw him or her to himself. Then it is up to that person to respond to God's work in his or her life.

Prayer and Fasting

Fasting is an important part of prayer throughout Scripture. Jesus seemed to assume that his followers would fast after he left them. Here are some biblical principles about fasting.

- Fast as you make a request to God (2 Sam. 12:23; Ezra 8:21).
- Fast as you seek the Lord about an issue or concern (2 Chron. 20:3; Esther 4:1–3; Dan. 6:18).
- Fast in order to humble yourself before God (Ezra 8:21; Ps. 69:10–11; Isa. 58:3).
- Fast as an expression of repentance (Ezra 9:5; Neh. 1:4–11, 9:1; Jer. 36:4–8; Dan. 9:3; Joel 1:14, 2:12–14).
- Fast as you pray for others in need (Esther 4:16; Ps. 35:13; Acts 14:23).
- Fast as you prepare for an important event (Esther 4:16; Acts 13:2–3).
- Fast for God's reward, not man's (Matt. 6:16–18).
- Fast when commissioning and appointing God's people for ministry (Acts 13:2–3, 14:23).
- Fasting is a way of having your prayers heard by God (Isa. 58:4; Matt. 9:14; Mark 2:18–20; Luke 5:33–35).
- Fasting is a way to submit to God, not a way to get what you want (Isa. 58:3).
- Fasting is not as important as repentance and righteousness (Isa. 58:6–9; Luke 18:12).
- Fasting is a form of worship (Luke 2:37; Acts 13:2–3).
- Fasting can be a time of rejoicing in the blessings of God and a time to seek him and his favor (Zech. 8:18–23).
- Fasting is a normal part of the Christian life (Matt. 6:16–18).
- Fasting is a part of life for those in covenant with Jesus until his return (Matt. 9:14; Mark 2:18–20; Luke 5:33–35).
- There are many forms of fasting:
    - Individuals fast for multiple days (Neh. 1:4–11).
    - A group of assembled people fast together (Neh. 9:1).

- People fast while performing other acts of humility, such as reading Scripture, praying with a loud voice, standing and praising (Neh. 9:1), weeping (Ps. 69:10–11), and bowing (Isa. 58:5).
- Some fast by neither eating nor drinking (Esther 4:16).
- Some fast in community with others (Jer. 36:4–8).

You probably have a lot of questions about fasting. Don't feel like you have to have all the answers before getting started. The most important thing is to do it! Here is a suggestion to get started: skip lunch one day a week. During that lunch hour, get alone with God and pray. Continue in your fasting journey by studying more about fasting in Scripture and other books. Ask God to lead you in the ways he wants you to fast.

I want to point out one principle that I found striking as I studied fasting in the Bible. One of the most prominent reasons for fasting was to express repentance. I encourage you to fast in a specific way for a particular period of time, especially if there is sin in your life for which you need to confess and repent. This is not a way of punishing or cleansing yourself; the blood of Jesus does that! Fasting is taking a specific action of faith and obedience as a sign of your repentance.

Discussion Questions

- What are the four basic aspects of prayer?
- Do you struggle to stay focused while you pray? What are you distracted by?
- What are some effective strategies for staying focused while you pray? Which of these sound the most helpful to you?
- How can we know that God will answer our prayers?
- How can we know we are praying according to God's will?
- Will you consider fasting sometime?

Big Ideas

- Four basic aspects of prayer include worship, confession, intercession for others, and personal requests.
- Here are some effective strategies for staying focused while you pray:
    - Pray the Bible.
    - Pray out loud.
    - Use prayer postures.
    - Pray about whatever is on your mind.
    - Make a to-do list.
    - Practice stillness, quietness, and focus.
    - Take a walk.
- The key to having confidence that God will hear and answer specific prayers is that we are asking according to his will.
- To get started with fasting, you could skip lunch one day a week. During that lunch hour, get alone with God and pray.

For Further Reading

Frizzell, Gregory. 1999. *How to Have a Powerful Prayer Life: The Biblical Path to Holiness and Relationship with God*. Memphis: The Master Design.

Eastman, Dick. 1978. *The Hour That Changes the World: A Practical Plan for Personal Prayer*. Grand Rapids: Baker Books.

CHAPTER 8

Living in Victory

—⁓—

I WAS A YOUNG MAN when I became the new pastor of a small, rural Baptist church. Soon after my arrival, I went to visit the home of the chairman of the deacons. Seated in his living room, I noticed that he was chewing and spitting tobacco into a cup.

The lead deacon of my new church explained, "I hope you don't mind if I chew. I know I shouldn't, but everyone has something. This is mine."

This man's statement was striking because it revealed what he believed. I have found this type of thinking in many Christians. The line of reasoning goes something like this:

"We all have sin and will keep on sinning. Nobody is perfect." This then leads to another conclusion: "I don't expect anyone to be perfect, and I should not be expected to be perfect, either." The final step in this logic, as this deacon succinctly expressed, is that we have a right to cherish a sin—to justify and keep it. He had concluded that it was wrong for him to chew tobacco, but he chose to continue to do it because he should not be expected to be perfect.

There is another line of thinking that practically brings us to the same conclusion. It is this: "Growing as a Christian is a journey and a process. We call it sanctification. I cannot be expected to stop all the sins in my life at once. It will take time." We then make a list of the things we hope to do better as Christians...one day. We have then falsely appeased our consciences and convinced ourselves that we have responded to the conviction of God. The result is the same: we knowingly allow sin to remain in our lives. The main point of this chapter is to help you understand that this is unbiblical thinking and practice. God has set us free from sin!

Freedom from Sin

We have already covered some important ideas related to living in victory. In the first chapter, we came to understand that we are hopelessly trapped in sin without Christ and that we deserve punishment. The first step to freedom is to understand that the death of Christ on the cross completely paid for our sins and thus removed our punishment. We have also understood that as God convicts us of sin, the only appropriate response is to confess our sin and repent.

Are we then left with the belief that although our sins are paid for, we are destined to be enslaved to it until Jesus returns? Let's see what the Bible teaches. This is a long passage, but please read it carefully:

What shall we say then? Are we to continue in sin that grace may abound?
By no means! How can we who died to sin still live in it?
Do you not know that all of us who have been baptized
into Christ Jesus were baptized into his death?
We were buried therefore with him by baptism into death, in order that,
just as Christ was raised from the dead by the glory of the Father,
we too might walk in newness of life.
For if we have been united with him in a death like his,
we shall certainly be united with him in a resurrection like his.
We know that our old self was crucified with him
in order that the body of sin might be brought to nothing,
so that we would no longer be enslaved to sin.
For one who has died has been set free from sin.
Now if we have died with Christ, we believe that we will also live with him.
We know that Christ, being raised from the dead, will never die again;
death no longer has dominion over him.
For the death he died he died to sin, once for all, but the life he lives he lives to God.
So you also must consider yourselves dead to sin and alive to God in Christ Jesus.
Let not sin therefore reign in your mortal body, to make you obey its passions.
Do not present your members to sin as instruments for unrighteousness,
but present yourselves to God as those who have been brought from death to life,
and your members to God as instruments for righteousness.

For sin will have no dominion over you, since you are not under law but under grace.
Romans 6:1–14

When we are united with Jesus Christ by faith, we take part in his death and resurrection. We take part in his death because our old, sinful selves have died. We take part in his resurrection because, with Christ, we are given new life. If we are united with Christ, then sin, which is part of our old life, has no place. We are set free from enslavement to sin.

How do we make this teaching a reality in our lives? First, we must *know* that we are free from sin. Paul writes, "Do you not know..." (Rom. 6:3). Many Christians continue to allow sin in their lives because they are not taught this biblical truth regarding our victory in Christ. The first step, then, is to learn the truth that God's Word teaches concerning our freedom from sin. Do you understand what Paul is teaching in Romans 6 about freedom from sin?

Next, we *believe* that we are free from sin. Paul writes,

You also must consider yourselves dead to sin and alive to God in Christ Jesus.
Romans 6:11

Not only must we know this truth, we must consider (or believe) it to be true. Do you consider yourself to be dead to sin and alive to God? This is not easy when we sometimes feel helpless against the power of sin. But you must choose either to believe the lie that you are helpless against sin or to believe that God has given you power over sin. You can take God at his Word!

The final step is to *act* on the reality now received.

Let not sin therefore reign in your mortal body.
Romans 6:12

Simply do not allow it. Some may respond, "But I don't have the power to resist sin. It is too strong." Well, then, we must go back to step two. Believe that in Christ you are dead to sin and alive to God. God has, in fact, set you free from sin! You will be amazed at the simplicity of this when you receive this powerful truth and act on it. You will see the supposed power of sin vanish like a vapor.

> You will see the supposed power of sin vanish like a vapor.

This is not to say that we do not have sinful desires (what the Bible calls the desires of the flesh). They are real. They will certainly try to pull you in the direction of sin. James explains what happens:

But each person is tempted when he is lured and enticed by his own desire.
Then desire when it has conceived gives birth to sin,
and sin when it is fully grown brings forth death.
James 1:14–15

Paul also describes how the desires of the flesh pull against the Spirit.

But I say, walk by the Spirit, and you will not gratify the desires of the flesh.
For the desires of the flesh are against the Spirit,
and the desires of the Spirit are against the flesh,
for these are opposed to each other,
to keep you from doing the things you want to do...
But the fruit of the Spirit is love, joy, peace, patience, kindness,
goodness, faithfulness, gentleness, self-control;
against such things there is no law.
And those who belong to Christ Jesus have crucified the flesh
with its passions and desires.
Galatians 5:16–17, 22–24

While we do have sinful desires, they are only desires. It was an important discovery for me when I realized that my will is not the same as my desires. This means that I am able to choose to do something different than that which I desire to do. Our culture has taught us that we must do what we desire to do. This is consistent with the former reality of our enslavement to sin. But if we are in Christ, this is no longer true about us. We may look squarely at the strong and real desire that burns in us and say, "No!" The desire is there, but it is not our master.

In addition to our crucified flesh and new life, there is even more assurance of our victory over sin. We do not face the temptation on our own. Christ himself, by his Holy Spirit, lives in us! What an incredible, empowering truth!

I have been crucified with Christ.
It is no longer I who live, but Christ who lives in me.
And the life I now live in the flesh I live by faith in the Son of God,
who loved me and gave himself for me.
Galatians 2:20

God has also promised his grace for power to do his will.

But by the grace of God I am what I am, and his grace toward me was not in vain.
On the contrary, I worked harder than any of them,
though it was not I, but the grace of God that is with me.
1 Corinthians 15:10

And God is able to make all grace abound to you,
so that having all sufficiency in all things at all times,
you may abound in every good work.
2 Corinthians 9:8

God has promised to give us *everything* we need in *every* situation in *every* moment to do what is right. On what basis, then, can we continue in the belief that we are not free from sin? In fact,

If we say we have fellowship with him while we walk in darkness,
we lie and do not practice the truth.
1 John 1:6

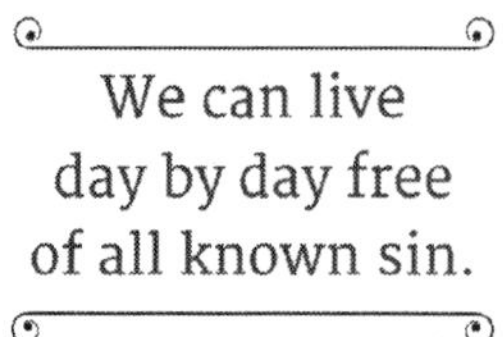
We can live
day by day free
of all known sin.

Now, here is a common question: "So are you saying we can live perfectly in this life?" No, I don't believe we will be perfect in the true, moral sense until Jesus comes back. I continue to find layers of selfishness and pride in my mind and heart of which I was not aware. But let me be clear: we can live victoriously! We always have the power not to sin. We have no excuses. We can live day by day, free of all known sin. Any and every sin that God brings to my consciousness can be confessed, repented of, and removed from my life by faith in the Gospel and the present power of the Holy Spirit!

The Spiritual Battle

We have already identified a hindrance to living in victory: our own sinful desires. Sometimes the Bible calls this "the flesh." There are two other significant challenges to living in victory: the world and the spiritual forces of evil.

By "the world," I do not mean the earth, which is God's good creation. "The world" refers to the lifestyles and cultures of the people who are in rebellion against God. Here is a description of how the world works:

And you were dead in the trespasses and sins in which you once walked,
following the course of this world, following the prince of the power of the air,
the spirit that is now at work in the sons of disobedience
—among whom we all once lived in the passions of our flesh,
carrying out the desires of the body and the mind,
and were by nature children of wrath, like the rest of mankind.
Ephesians 2:1–3

The course of the world is led by Satan ("the prince of the power of the air"), who works in those who disobey God and give in to the desires of the flesh. We don't just have our own wrong desires to deal with; we also live in a world that is filled with people and cultures who obey their wrong desires. So we are warned to keep ourselves free from the influence of the world.

Do not love the world or the things in the world.
If anyone loves the world, the love of the Father is not in him.
For all that is in the world—
the desires of the flesh and the desires of the eyes and pride of life—
is not from the Father but is from the world.
And the world is passing away along with its desires,
but whoever does the will of God abides forever.
1 John 2:15–17

Do not be conformed to this world, but be transformed by the renewal of your mind,
that by testing you may discern what is the will of God,
what is good and acceptable and perfect.
Romans 12:2

Satan not only leads the world, he is also the leader of the spiritual forces of evil. The Bible teaches that there are spiritual beings created by God (as angels) who have rebelled against God and are waging war on God's people in order to frustrate God's purposes.

For we do not wrestle against flesh and blood,
but against the rulers, against the authorities,
against the cosmic powers over this present darkness,
against the spiritual forces of evil in the heavenly places.
Ephesians 6:12

Satan and his army tempt, accuse, scare, and lie to us. What God's people must understand is that Jesus Christ has given us certain and eternal victory over these forces. We have nothing to fear! On the cross, Jesus "disarmed the rulers and authorities and put them to open shame, by triumphing over them in him" (Col. 2:15). Paul prayed that the Ephesians would understand:

What is the immeasurable greatness of his power toward us who believe,
according to the working of his great might
that he worked in Christ when he raised him from the dead

and seated him at his right hand in the heavenly places,
far above all rule and authority and power and dominion,
and above every name that is named,
not only in this age but also in the one to come.
Ephesians 1:19–21

In fact, God "raised us up with him and seated us with him in the heavenly places in Christ Jesus" (Eph. 2:6). Consider Paul's description of the certainty of our victory and unity with Christ and his love:

If God is for us, who can be against us?
Who shall bring any charge against God's elect?
Who shall separate us from the love of Christ?
Shall tribulation, or distress, or persecution,
or famine, or nakedness, or danger, or sword?
No, in all these things we are more than conquerors through him who loved us.
For I am sure that neither death nor life, nor angels nor rulers,
nor things present nor things to come, nor powers,
nor height nor depth, nor anything else in all creation,
will be able to separate us from the love of God in Christ Jesus our Lord.
Romans 8:31b, 33a, 35, 37–39

Many who claim to follow Jesus live defeated lives. They live subjected to sin, the world, and evil spirits. One reason is that they are not aware of the spiritual battle that is taking place. Another reason is that they are not aware that God has given them freedom and victory over these enemies. When we understand these things, we can let Jesus live his life and power through us by faith!

Overcoming Bondage and Bad Habits

Do you feel like you are stuck in sin? Have you established deep habits of sin that seem too difficult to break free from? Have you fallen into addictions to food, sex, or drugs? These are strongholds in your life that can be broken through Christ!

Some believers are even under the influence of evil spirits, even though most in our Western culture are not aware of it. The primary strategy of evil spirits is to tell us lies. Sometimes these lies become regular patterns of our thinking that are difficult to change. These strongholds in your life can also be broken through Christ!

If you feel you are stuck in sin or under the influence of the world or evil spirits, consider these paths to victory.

- Follow the instructions for getting right with God in chapter 2. If you need to, find someone to help you go through it. You may find it is too difficult to do it by yourself. Hopefully, you can think of a believer in your life whom you can ask to help you. Maybe you have parents or a pastor who can help you. If you feel that you have no one at all, please contact me so that I can help you find someone. You can e-mail me at matthew@truthtofreedom.org.
- Read *The Bondage Breaker*, by Neil Anderson, and go through the "Seven Steps to Freedom." Again, you may need to find someone to help you go through this. Anyone in your family or church can read the book and go through the steps with you. It is helpful just to have someone there with you, praying for you. There are also trained helpers from Freedom in Christ Ministries. You can search your area on this website: ficm.org/find-help.
- If you are struggling with addiction, please find help with the particular area you are dealing with. For example, Hebron Colony Ministry (hebroncolony.org) is a ministry in our area that helps men struggling with substance abuse. There are other ministries like this, centered on biblical principles, that can help you gain freedom from addiction.
- It is critical that you find a church so that you can benefit from biblical teaching, fellowship, accountability, and personal discipleship. Please see chapter 11 for more on this topic.

- Most importantly, seek to develop a personal relationship with Jesus Christ by walking with him throughout the day and spending time with him in prayer and the Word. We cannot do it on our own! Jesus invites us to live in him so that we can bear much fruit.

Abide in me, and I in you.
As the branch cannot bear fruit by itself, unless it abides in the vine,
neither can you, unless you abide in me.
I am the vine; you are the branches.
Whoever abides in me and I in him, he it is that bears much fruit,
for apart from me you can do nothing.
John 15:4–5

Discussion Questions

- Before reading this chapter, what was your understanding of sin in the life of the Christian?
- Do you understand what Paul is teaching in Romans 6 about freedom from sin?
- Do you believe that God has set you free from sin?
- Why are we able to overcome sin in our lives?
- Are you aware of the spiritual battle in your life?
- Do you feel like you are stuck in sin? Have you established deep habits of sin that seem too difficult to break free from? Have you fallen into addictions to food, sex, or drugs?
- Will you take the steps provided here for overcoming bondages and bad habits?

Big Ideas

- If we are united with Christ, then sin, which is part of our old life, has no place. We are set free from enslavement to sin.

- How do we make this teaching a reality in our lives?
    - We must *know* that we are free from sin.
    - We *believe* that we are free from sin.
    - We *act* on the reality that we are free from sin.
- We may look squarely at the strong and real desires that burn in us and say, "No!" The desires are there, but they are not our masters.
- God has promised to give us *everything* we need in *every* situation in *every* moment to do what is right.
- "The world" refers to the lifestyles and cultures of the people who are in rebellion against God.
- Satan and his army tempt, accuse, scare, and lie to us. What God's people must understand is that Jesus Christ has given us certain and eternal victory over these forces.

For Further Reading

Anderson, Neil T. 2000. *The Bondage Breaker: Overcoming Negative Thoughts, Irrational Feelings, Habitual Sins.* Eugene, Oregon: Harvest House Publishers.

CHAPTER 9

Ministering to Others

I REMEMBER THE FIRST TIME I ever told Dana that I loved her. It was not very romantic. Now, we have had plenty of romantic times, but this was not one of them. We were unmarried and still in college. We were late coming into church one Sunday evening, and I stopped her in the foyer when no one was around. I turned her toward me and said, "I love you. I don't mean that I'm in love with you (which I am). I mean that I am committed to doing what is best for you. I am committed to that." It was totally spontaneous, and I meant it. I have been trying to live that out for the last twenty-two years.

Remember that amazing question the scribe asked Jesus? Do you remember his answer?

"Which commandment is the most important of all?"
Jesus answered, "The most important is,
'Hear, O Israel: The Lord our God, the Lord is one.
And you shall love the Lord your God
with all your heart and with all your soul
and with all your mind and with all your strength.'"
Mark 12:30

But Jesus didn't stop there. He added a bonus answer.

"The second is this: 'You shall love your neighbor as yourself.'
There is no other commandment greater than these.
Mark 12:31

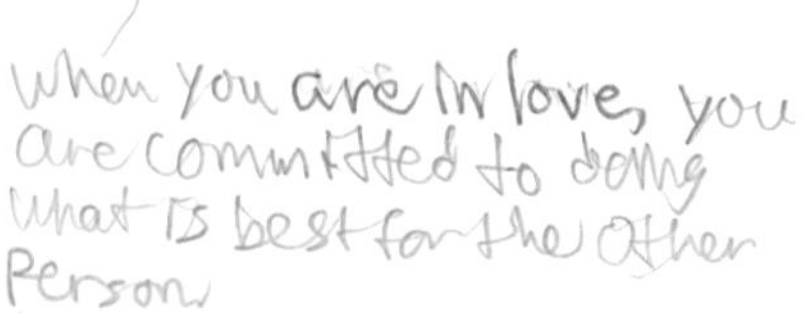

When you are in love, you
are committed to doing
what is best for the other
person

Jesus also connects these two commandments. He explains that loving others is essential to loving God:

As the Father has loved me, so have I loved you. Abide in my love.
If you keep my commandments, you will abide in my love,
just as I have kept my Father's commandments and abide in his love…
This is my commandment, that you love one another as I have loved you.
John 15:9–12

Anyone who does not love does not know God, because God is love…
If anyone says, "I love God," and hates his brother, he is a liar;
for he who does not love his brother whom he has seen
cannot love God whom he has not seen.
And this commandment we have from him:
whoever loves God must also love his brother.
1 John 4:8, 20–21

What does it mean to love others? This is an important question because our culture uses the word *love* with such varying and casual meanings. "I love ice cream!" "I love football!" "I love fishing!" "I love my wife!" In fact, just this week I told my wife that I loved her, and she asked me, "What do you mean by that?" I'm pretty sure my wife wants me to love her in a different way than I love ice cream.

Our culture talks about being *in love.* When we say that we are in love, we are talking about how we feel, how much we like someone or something. Unfortunately, this is exactly *not* what love is, according to the Bible. Love is self-sacrifice for the good of another person.

Greater love has no one than this,
that someone lay down his life for his friends.
John 15:13

Love is patient and kind; love does not envy or boast; it is not arrogant or rude.
It does not insist on its own way; it is not irritable or resentful.
1 Corinthians 13:4–5

Love has nothing to do with how we feel. In fact, love is what we do *in spite of* how we may feel. Love has nothing to do with what we get out of it. Real love is about giving, not getting. Jesus said:

> *For if you love those who love you, what reward do you have?*
> *Do not even the tax collectors do the same?*
> *And if you greet only your brothers, what more are you doing than others?*
> *Do not even the Gentiles do the same?*
> Matthew 5:46–47

The world and Satan try to convince us that if we get what we want, we will be happy. This is a lie. While we may be happy in the sense of temporary pleasure, selfishness actually does not lead us to fulfillment and joy. When we deny ourselves and love God, we find that he is all we ever needed or wanted. In the same way, when we deny ourselves and love others, we find joy and satisfaction.

A Call to Ministry

If you grew up in church, you have probably heard the phrase *called to ministry*. A call is a task given to us by God. This phrase is usually applied to pastors, missionaries, and other vocational ministers. One of the most unfortunate developments of the modern church is the belief that only certain Christians are called to ministry. Many believers have the idea that they are like consumers or clients who come to church to get their spiritual needs met. They think pastors and missionaries are the ones responsible to reach the world for Christ. After all, that is what we pay them to do.

> Selfishness actually does not lead us to fulfillment and joy.

Some are indeed called to be pastors, missionaries, church leaders, and vocational ministers. But these leaders are not the only ministers. In fact, it is their responsibility to equip all Christians for ministry. The Bible explains their job:

And he gave the apostles, the prophets, the evangelists, the shepherds and teachers, to equip the saints for the work of ministry, for building up the body of Christ.
Ephesians 4:11–12

The saints refers to all believers in Jesus Christ. This passage indicates that all believers are to be equipped for the work of ministry. *Saint* means holy person, someone set apart for God's purpose. Since God's purpose for us is to love him and to love people, we are all called to ministry. *You* are called to ministry!

Ministry is when someone serves others to bless or benefit them in some way. In God's economy, a servant is the greatest of all.

Whoever would be great among you must be your servant,
and whoever would be first among you must be your slave,
even as the Son of Man came not to be served but to serve,
and to give his life as a ransom for many.
Matthew 20:26b–28

Another way we know that God has called us to ministry is that he has given every believer particular abilities for serving others that are empowered by the Holy Spirit.

Now concerning spiritual gifts, brothers, I do not want you to be uninformed...
To each is given the manifestation of the Spirit for the common good...
All these are empowered by one and the same Spirit,
who apportions to each one individually as he wills.
1 Corinthians 12:1, 7, 11

So if you are a believer, then you have already been given spiritual abilities (or gifts). God chose to give you these gifts, which are empowered by the Holy Spirit, for the purpose of building up the body of Christ.

What are these gifts? In 1 Corinthians 12, Paul mentions these: the utterance of wisdom; the utterance of knowledge; faith; healing; miracles; prophecy; the ability to distinguish between spirits; tongues; and the interpretation of tongues. There are other passages that mention these and other spiritual gifts: teaching; serving; exhorting; giving; leading; mercy (Rom. 12:6–8); apostleship; helping; administration (1 Cor. 12:28); and evangelism and shepherding (Eph. 4:11).

How do we know what gifts God has given us? There are many "spiritual gift tests" out there that may help you begin to narrow it down. However, I would like to suggest that knowing what your spiritual gift is isn't nearly as important as using it. But how can you use it if you don't know what it is? God has already given it to you, so the best thing to do is to look around you for needs in others' lives and get busy trying to meet them. Even our observation of people's needs helps us understand our gifting. People with different gifts see different needs because of the perspective their gifts give them. For example, someone with the gift of teaching may see the gaps in the biblical understanding of his brothers and sisters in Christ, while someone with the gift of mercy may be more sensitive to the hurts and troubles of those around him.

Therefore, one of the best ways to discover your gift is to get busy ministering to others. Another way is to observe the effectiveness and personal satisfaction that result from your ministry. There is great joy and fullness of the Spirit when he uses you to build others up! You can also ask other believers around you to give you feedback on the strengths they see in your life as you minister.

There are many ways to minister to people. We can minister to them *physically*. Some people need clothes, food, and shelter. Some need a helping hand, material provision, or healing. We can minister to people *emotionally*. Many need affirmation, encouragement, friendship, and comfort. We can minister to people *spiritually*. Everyone needs wisdom and instruction about how to love God. Helping people to love God is the best way we can love and minister to them! This is what it means to make disciples.

Making Disciples

This brings us from the Great Commandment to the Great Commission. The last thing that Jesus said to his disciples before he returned to heaven was this:

> *All authority in heaven and on earth has been given to me.*
> *Go therefore and make disciples of all nations,*
> *baptizing them in the name of the Father*
> *and of the Son and of the Holy Spirit,*
> *teaching them to observe all that I have commanded you.*
> *And behold, I am with you always, to the end of the age.*
> Matthew 28:18–20

A disciple is a student or follower of someone. Jesus wants us to help others become his followers. This is the most important way that we can love and minister to others. Let's look at what we can learn about our mission from these verses.

God has given us authority to make disciples. What Jesus says about himself in verse 18 is powerful! He has been given all authority in heaven and on earth. Therefore, as he commissions us, we are authorized by God to carry out his instructions.

We don't have to apologize or be concerned about disrupting people's lives. Their Creator told us to invite them to follow him! We don't need permission from anyone but Jesus. The world, the culture, and the government may tell us we can't tell others about Jesus, but we don't have to listen to them. We *cannot* listen to them. We are under orders from the supreme authority!

> God has given us authority to make disciples.

God has called us to engage the world intentionally in our everyday lives. The main verb of verse 19 is *make.* The other verbs give further explanation about making disciples. These modifying verbs (which are all participles in the Greek) are *going, baptizing,* and *teaching.* In his book *Making Friends for Christ*, Wayne McDill (my dad!) suggests that *going* emphasizes intentionality and penetration:

> This "Going" pictures the mobility of the church as a part of the flow of the world's traffic. Our task here calls for the *penetration* of the unbelieving community with our salt and light influence for Christ...In his "going" every Christian charts the boundaries of his

> own personal mission field. In these every-day contacts he is the key to the penetrating influences of the church.[9]

For some, *going* takes on a more radical application. We know that the scope of this disciple-making mission is global, because we are to make disciples *of all nations*. There are places in the world where people have not heard about Jesus or do not have the Bible in their own languages. The church is called to go to these places and make disciples. Some Christians leave their homes and travel to other parts of the world to reach people for Christ. Others are called to give financially and serve from home to support these missionaries.

Beyond the activity of *going*, there are two specific ways that we make disciples: *baptizing* and *teaching*. I will explain these two activities in the next two sections on evangelism and discipleship.

Evangelism

According to the Great Commission, evangelism is the first part of making disciples, "baptizing them in the name of the Father and the Son and the Holy Spirit" (Matt. 28:19b). Baptism is when a believer is symbolically immersed in water as a representation of his or her faith in Jesus Christ. I remember when my dad baptized me. It was a special time for me, as I expressed my faith and unity with Christ. My dad even used the phrase from these verses as he baptized me: "I baptize you in the name of the Father and the Son and the Holy Spirit."

We can get a basic idea of what the Bible teaches about baptism from the following verses.

1. The Bible teaches that believers are to be baptized (Matt. 28:18–20; Acts 8:36–38).
2. Baptism is a picture that reminds us of what happens to us when we give our lives to Jesus and become united with him (Gal. 3:26–27).
   - We are cleansed from the things we have done wrong and are forgiven by God (Acts 22:16).

- We have died with Jesus (our old life of sin is over) and have begun a new life of obedience (Rom. 6:1–7).
- We become a part of God's family (1 Cor. 12:13).
- God comes to live in us by the Holy Spirit to teach, lead, and give us strength (Acts 1:5).

In the Great Commission, baptism represents the task of bringing people to faith in Christ. We often call this task *evangelism*. The word *evangelism* comes from the Greek word *euangelion*, which means "good news," and is usually translated as *gospel* in the Bible. The verb *to evangelize* comes from the Greek verb *euangelizo*, which means "to bring or proclaim good news." We know that the Gospel (good news) in the Bible refers to the saving work of Jesus.

Now I would remind you, brothers, of the gospel I preached to you…
For I delivered to you as of first importance what I also received:
that Christ died for our sins in accordance with the Scriptures,
that he was buried, that he was raised on the third day
in accordance with the Scriptures.
1 Corinthians 15:1a, 3–4

Making Friends for Christ

There are many wonderful ways to introduce people to Jesus Christ. I would like to focus on one of the most natural and effective methods: *relational evangelism*. This is the what my dad suggests in his book, *Making Friends for Christ: A Practical Approach to Relational Evangelism*. He explains that our strategy for bringing people to Christ can reflect the strategy of God himself in Christ's mission. The ministry of Jesus was incarnational, relational, and intentional. For us, this means that we are present in the lives of those who are lost (incarnational), we are developing real friendships with them (relational), and we are deliberately introducing them to Christ (intentional).

Many Christians mainly have only friends who are Christians. They may interact with unbelievers when necessary at work or in public, but that is not the same as developing real friendships with them. We do not have to go to foreign countries or find unbelieving strangers to evangelize. The most effective strategy is to develop relationships with unbelievers you already know. God has given each of us a unique set of family members, neighbors, colleagues in business, and touch points in our public pathways. This is our mission field!

So how can we turn these acquaintances into friends? McDill shares a simple and powerful way: *by listening to them!* Listening demonstrates "your sincere interest in your neighbor's personal concerns."[10] When you listen to others, they sense that you care for them, and they learn to trust and open up to you. At the same time, you learn about their needs so that you can pray for and minister to them.

But they can't do all the talking! Another way to develop friendships is by sharing your own needs and experiences with others. Friendships deepen as both parties share about themselves. Generally, friends will get closer as they choose to talk about more real and personal subjects. As you open up to your friends, they will most likely open up to you.

As we have already established, the motivation for ministry is love. Our goal is not to meet our own needs but the needs of others. McDill presents four levels of love that will help us develop friendships for ministry. The first level of love is *acknowledgment*. This is the act of recognizing the presence of another person in a personal, genuine way. The next level is *acceptance*. McDill explains, "This has to do with receiving the person just as he is, without placing conditions he must meet to satisfy me."[11] The third level of love is *affirmation*. We affirm others when we choose to associate with them as friends. The final level of love is *atonement*. This is the most important kind of love, when we help others reconcile to God through Christ.

When you listen to others, they sense that you care for them and learn to trust and open up to you.

One of the most powerful ways we can show these levels of love is to invite others into our homes. As we invite others into our personal spaces, we are inviting them into our lives. In this context of hospitality, unbelievers get a glimpse of the Christian life and family. We often underestimate the power of simply allowing people to see the love and hope we have in Jesus. Sometimes when we invite people into our homes, we get caught up in wanting everything to be perfect or in worrying about how things look. But what we really want is for them to see what it means to follow Jesus in a real-life context.

Another effective piece of advice about evangelism in *Making Friends for Christ* is what Dad calls "The Three-Story Witness." This is a way to present the gospel by exploring three stories. The first story is the one your friend tells you about himself as you show genuine interest, listen, and ask questions. The second story is the one you tell about how God has saved you and changed your life. You can be prepared to share your testimony by writing it out ahead of time. Here is an outline you can follow:

- My life before knowing Christ as my Savior
- How I came to realize I needed Christ
- How I put my trust in Him
- How God has changed my life[12]

The final and most important story is the story of Jesus. There are many wonderful stories in the Bible about Jesus that will help others learn who he is. But the most important story is how he has saved us from our sins through his death, burial, and resurrection. Using this three-story witness allows you to move naturally in your relationships and conversations to the point that you can share the gospel with others.

Engaging the World with Wisdom and Courage

While we are making friends and sharing Christ, it is important that we remember that we are in a spiritual battle. Jesus said to his disciples:

> *Behold, I am sending you out as sheep in the midst of wolves,*
> *so be wise as serpents and innocent as doves.*
> Matthew 10:16

Paul also warned believers to be careful:

Do not be deceived: "Bad company ruins good morals."
1 Corinthians 15:33

So how do we help people to know Christ if it is dangerous to spend time with unbelievers? Throughout history, various strategies have been suggested to solve this problem. Those strategies can be grouped into four positions believers can take in relation to the world: isolation, protection, engagement, and partnership. The two extremes that must be avoided are *isolation* and *partnership*. Instead, we want to find a balance between *protection* and *engagement*.

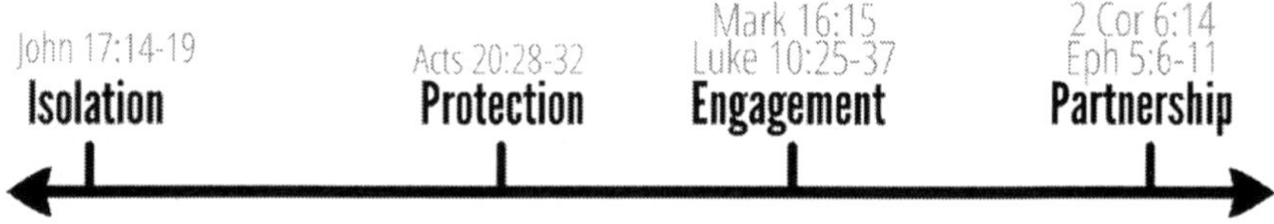

Even if we become friends with people who don't know Christ, Paul teaches that we are not to become *partners* with them (2 Cor. 6:14; Eph. 5:6–11). This means that we are not to form serious partnerships with them, such as marriage, and that we do not participate in any of their disobedient behavior.

In response to these warnings, some Christians *isolate* themselves from the world. But instead of taking us out of the world, Jesus sends us into the world and prays for our *protection*!

I have given them your word, and the world has hated them
because they are not of the world, just as I am not of the world.
I do not ask that you take them out of the world,
but that you keep them from the evil one.
They are not of the world, just as I am not of the world.
Sanctify them in the truth; your word is truth.

As you sent me into the world, so I have sent them into the world.
And for their sake I consecrate myself, that they also may be sanctified in truth.
John 17:14–18

This passage is a wonderful description of how we are to be pure and set apart from the evil of the world, and yet we are not isolated from the world. Instead, Jesus calls us to *engagement.*

The church can engage the world on many levels—culturally, legally, politically, and socially. All of these are important parts of the Christian's influence on the world. However, it is critical that we understand that the mission of the church is not to change the culture, laws, or political powers of the world. Influencing the world in these ways is right, and we should seek to establish righteousness and justice. But the church has often made the mistake of working much harder to change these things than to achieve its true mission of building the kingdom of God by making disciples. We can be sure that the most effective way to influence the culture, laws, or political powers of the world is to change hearts by leading people to Christ.

So as we engage the world, how do we do so in such a way that we are not morally corrupted (1 Cor. 15:33)? This question reflects the legitimate need of the believer for *protection* from the world. As we consider our relationships with others so that we stay engaged but also remain pure, there are three variables to consider: the quality of the relationship, the quantity of time spent together, and the direction of influence. By "quality of the relationship," I am referring to how intimate we are with others. Considering these aspects of friendship is particularly helpful as parents guide children in assessing their friendships.

The key variable is the direction of influence. Who seems to be exerting the most influence in the relationship? Sometimes this is difficult to evaluate. While both parties in a friendship will influence one another, the main question is whether your friend is drawing you into sin or causing too much temptation. Friendships that have potential for moral danger can be managed by reducing the intimacy or quantity of time together.

Another way in which we can find strength and protection as we engage the world is through our participation in the church. While it is great to have unbelieving friends, it is important for our closest friends to be fellow believers. We need to spend plenty of time with God's people. They can encourage us in our ministry and hold us accountable for our purity. We will discuss this important part of our lives in chapter 11.

In addition to moral danger, there are other dangers we face as we engage the world. The Bible warns us of rejection and persecution (Matt. 10:16–39). Fear of rejection and persecution is one of the primary obstacles of evangelism. Such fear is rooted in selfishness and pride and often prevents us from reaching out, making friends, and sharing Christ. We do not want to get hurt, to fail, or to be rejected. But, as we have already noted, following Jesus means denying ourselves. We have also observed that love means that we put the interests of others before our own. Those who have trusted Christ for salvation are even willing to sacrifice their own lives to acknowledge Christ before men.

And do not fear those who kill the body but cannot kill the soul.
Rather fear him who can destroy both soul and body in hell…
So everyone who acknowledges me before men,
I also will acknowledge before my Father who is in heaven,
but whoever denies me before men,
I also will deny before my Father who is in heaven.
Matthew 10:28, 32

Discipleship

Discipleship is the second part of making disciples according to the Great Commission: "Teaching them to observe all that I have commanded you" (Matt. 28:20a). Not only do we help people place their faith in Christ for salvation, we then teach these believers to walk in obedience to Christ's commands. Paul instructs Timothy on the pattern for discipleship multiplication in the church:

What you have heard from me in the presence of many witnesses
entrust to faithful men who will be able to teach others also.
2 Timothy 2:2

We know that pastors and teachers are responsible for teaching the church to follow Christ (Titus 1:9), that husbands and parents are to teach their families to follow Christ (Eph. 5:25–27, 6:4), and that older men and women are to teach younger men and women to follow Christ (Titus 2:2–8). Many of these contexts and relationships will be discussed in more detail in the next two chapters on living in community. Discipleship can take place in church, in small groups, and in one-on-one mentor relationships. While discipleship often occurs informally in everyday life, it is also important to be intentional about it.

At almost any point in our Christian walk, we will find ourselves on both sides of a discipleship relationship, as a disciple and as a mentor. So take the initiative and find an older or more experienced, godly person (or small group) to mentor you in the Christian life. If you don't know of any, ask God to help you find someone. You might hesitate to ask someone to mentor you, thinking that they would not be interested in meeting with you. But remember, people are usually more willing than we think, and it doesn't hurt to ask.

Also, seek out a younger or less experienced Christian that you can mentor. Try to meet on a regular basis to discuss and hold each other accountable for the basic aspects of Christian living. Since discipleship is the primary purpose of this book, you can use it as a tool to help you disciple others. Each subject is carefully chosen to provide the basic building blocks for how to follow Jesus.

Discussion Questions

- What does it mean to love someone?
- Who is called to ministry?
- How will you respond to God's call to ministry?
- How can we discover our spiritual gifts?
- What are the two aspects of making disciples from Matthew 28:18–20?
- What are some ways we can introduce people to Christ?
- When we engage the world, which words best describe the positions we should take: isolation, protection, engagement, and partnership?
- Are you willing to find a mentor and be a mentor?

Big Ideas

- Loving others is essential to loving God.
- We are all called to ministry.
- Jesus wants us to help others become his followers.
- God has given us authority to make disciples.
- God has called us to engage the world intentionally in our everyday lives.
- Baptism is when a believer is symbolically immersed in water as a representation of his or her faith in Jesus as Savior and Lord.
- Evangelism is the task of bringing people to faith in Christ. Relational evangelism is one of the most natural and effective methods to introduce people to Jesus Christ.
- When relating to the world, there are four positions believers can take: isolation, protection, engagement, and partnership. The two extremes that must be avoided are isolation and partnership. Instead, we want to find a balance between protection and engagement.
- We need to spend plenty of time with God's people.
- Not only do we help people place their faith in Christ for salvation, we then teach these believers to walk in obedience to Christ's commands.
- At almost any point in our Christian walk, we will find ourselves on both sides of a discipleship relationship, as a disciple and as a mentor.

For Further Reading

McDill, Wayne. 2010. *Making Friends for Christ: A Practical Approach to Relational Evangelism*, 2nd ed. USA: Xulon Press.

CHAPTER 10

Living in Community—Family

—~—

IMAGINE A LARGE, SOLITARY EYEBALL—DISTURBING, I know. I wonder if Paul was trying to be humorous with this outrageous idea: What "if the whole body were an eye…" (1 Cor. 12:17)?

Or what if the eyeball of a certain body began to criticize the hand of his body? "I don't need you; I will get along just fine without you." I'm guessing that the eye is going to see a lot of wonderful things to touch and do. Seeing is awesome, but only seeing is not enough. I certainly would not choose to be blind, but would I choose instead to have my sight and be paralyzed?

Paul used this analogy to help believers understand that we need each other, that God does not intend for us to operate independently. We are like different parts of the human body. All the parts are important for functioning at our highest potential. No part survives on its own.

So God gives us families, churches, and communities. Learning to love God includes learning how he wants us to function and accomplish his mission in these various communities. Proverbs 18:1 explains that anyone who refuses to operate in community is being selfish and is rejecting the wisdom of learning from others.

Whoever isolates himself seeks his own desire.
He breaks out against all sound judgment.
Proverbs 18:1

In this chapter and the next, we will talk about the biblical principles related to living in community. We will start with the foundational principle of submission and then explore the relationships we have within marriage, parenting, and the church. Finally, we will discuss biblical conflict resolution.

Submission

One day, there was a huge fight taking place in my house. It seemed that every family member was involved. So I called a cease-fire and invited everyone to peace talks. We sat down in the living room, and I read this single question from James 4:1:

What causes quarrels and what causes fights among you?

What a simple and powerful question! If we could understand the cause of our fights, maybe we could prevent them from happening. James goes on to explain:

Is it not this, that your passions are at war within you?
You desire and do not have, so you murder.
You covet and cannot obtain, so you fight and quarrel.
You do not have, because you do not ask.
You ask and do not receive, because you ask wrongly,
to spend it on your passions. You adulterous people!
Do you not know that friendship with the world is enmity with God?
Therefore whoever wishes to be a friend of the world makes himself an enemy of God.
Or do you suppose it is to no purpose that the Scripture says,
"He yearns jealously over the spirit that he has made to dwell in us"?
But he gives more grace. Therefore it says,
"God opposes the proud, but gives grace to the humble."
Submit yourselves therefore to God.
Resist the devil, and he will flee from you.
James 4:1–7

In chapter 8, we discussed our three main enemies for living in freedom. Each one appears in this passage:

1) "your passions…within you…you desire…you covet;"
2) "the world;" and
3) "the devil."

James teaches that these desires, systems, and spirits that oppose God destroy relationships. He exhorts us to turn to God with our needs, to refuse to align ourselves with the world, and to resist the devil. This can all be summarized this way: "Submit yourselves therefore to God" (James 4:7a). So the first way we can avoid conflicts with other is to entrust our desires and needs to God.

Not only are we called to submit to God, but we are also called to submit to each other in various ways. Submission is the key to functioning well in any community or relationship. Submission is when one person yields to another person. When two cars are headed for the same lane at the same time, if one driver doesn't yield, there is going to be a wreck. In the same way, when one person isn't willing to yield in a conflict, there is going to be a fight. The second way, then, that we can avoid conflicts with others is to learn to submit to them in the right ways. The Bible reveals at least three important reasons we ought to submit to one another: love, truth, and authority.

Submission is the key to functioning well in any community or relationship.

1. *Love: We submit to one another because we want what is best for each other.* Love is when we sacrifice ourselves for the good of another. This means that we are yielding our own wills and desires for the benefit of someone else. We must understand, though, that loving others is not trying to make them happy by giving them what they *want.* Remember, getting what we want will not make us happy in the long run. Instead, loving others means giving them what they *need.* So when we submit to one another in love, we are putting someone else's needs, as defined by Scripture, before our own desires and needs.

Do nothing from selfish ambition or conceit,
but in humility count others more significant than yourselves.

Let each of you look not only to his own interests, but also to the interests of others.
Philippians 2:3–4

2. *Truth: We submit to one another when we speak what is true and right to each other.* When truth is delivered to us by any human agent, it is our responsibility to submit to it. Over and over in Scripture, we are instructed to teach, correct, warn, exhort, encourage, and remind one another of the truth. "Speaking the truth in love" is central to the function and growth of the body of Christ (see Eph. 4:11–16). Jesus gives authority to the individual believer, and to the church as a whole, to call our brothers and sisters to repentance from sin (Matt. 18:15–17).
3. *Authority: We submit to those to whom God has given the responsibility to lead.* God has given each of us particular roles in our various communities. Some are given the authority to lead and others the responsibility to follow. In marriage, the husband is given authority to lead, and the wife is called to follow (Eph. 5:22–33). In the family, parents are given the authority to train and discipline their children, and the children are responsible to obey (Eph. 6:1–4). In the church, elders are given the authority to teach, care for, and lead God's people (Acts 20:28). The church is responsible to follow their lead (Heb. 13:17). In the world, there are people with authority to lead in our employment (Eph. 6:5–8) and in the state (Rom. 13:1–7). These roles of authority will be touched on in the following discussion of the various communities in which we live. The important thing is to realize that if God has given someone authority to lead us, then our job is to submit to their leadership.

Have you already considered how countercultural all of this sounds? Our culture encourages self-gratification and individualism instead of love. Dominated by secularism, our culture has difficulty acknowledging that truth even exists. Since there are no absolutes, everyone is entitled to his or her own truth. In addition, our culture values autonomy to such a degree that almost every God-given authority is rejected.

But what if we did things God's way? What would our relationships look like if we submitted to one another in love and truth, and if we submitted to those in authority? Imagine each of us looking out for the interests of those around us instead of our own. Imagine each of us listening to others when they are helping us get on the right path. Imagine each of us faithfully following those who have authority to lead. If we all lived in this way, there would be significantly more peace. In addition, our relationships would be transformed, and we would enjoy the blessing and power of God in our communities.

Now let's take a look at how these principles work out in our relationships as husbands and wives, and as parents and children.

Marriage

A married couple is the first, smallest, and most basic community. This was a part of God's good plan from the very beginning.

Then the LORD God said, "It is not good that the man should be alone;
I will make him a helper fit for him."
Therefore a man shall leave his father and his mother
and hold fast to his wife, and they shall become one flesh.
Genesis 2:18, 24

Unmarried Believers

Most believers spend the majority of their lives married. Those who are not married either have not yet married, are called to be unmarried, or have lost their marriage partners. The most important thing to understand is that no matter what marital status we are in, our purpose and mission remain the same. We are to love God, love people, and make disciples, whether we are married or not. In addition, our purpose and the goals of our mission are eternal, while marriage is not. This should help us get a proper perspective on marriage; sometimes we make it more important than it really is.

So if you are currently unmarried, don't be concerned about it. If God wants you to marry, he will lead you and provide a partner for you. Wait on the Lord. In the meantime, focus all your attention on loving God and pursuing his call for your life!

While it is not necessary to be married in order to fulfill our purpose in life, the Bible teaches that marriage is a central part of God's overall strategy for accomplishing his purposes on the earth. For example, two of the most important functions of marriage are to create human life and to pass on love for God (Mal. 2:15). We will talk about this more in the next section on parenting. Since marriage is central to God's mission, the church needs to understand how to respond to our culture's current attack on this important relationship.

Marriage is a central part of God's overall strategy for accomplishing his purposes on the earth.

The Cultural Attack on Marriage

What does our culture say about marriage? According to the most recent moral developments, we don't really need marriage at all. We can have sexual intimacy with multiple partners outside of marriage. Divorce is normal and acceptable. Men can marry men, and women can marry women.

But *God* says that marriage is good and necessary for most people (Gen. 2:18, 24). God says that sexual intimacy should take place only within the context of a marriage between one woman and one man, who are married for life (Matt. 19:4–5; Eph. 5:3; Heb. 13:4). To the extent that our state and national laws do not reflect God's principles for marriage, we forsake the blessings of God. But regardless of what the government and culture do, our responsibility is to teach God's design and purpose for marriage in our homes and churches.

A more subtle way that the culture has twisted our understanding of marriage is to make it a means of selfish fulfillment. Even in the church, many believers seem to think that the primary purpose of marriage is to make us happy. Therefore, many

> Our goal is not to make our spouse happy, but to make him or her holy.

go into marriage thinking that their new partners will give them what they want and make them happy. The reality of marriage is often a rude awakening for those who get married with these expectations.

Jesus First in Marriage

Our couch is broken because it was used as a trampoline. Our broom is broken because it was used as a pole vault. Our wall has a hole in it because it was used as the rope in a boxing match. I am trying to teach my children that if you use an object for a purpose for which it was not intended, it usually breaks.

Our culture has turned marriage into something it was not intended to be. People are using it to accomplish something it wasn't intended to accomplish. Just like the objects in my home, marriages will break when we are not honoring God's design and purpose for it. God never intended for us to seek happiness and fulfillment in marriage. We are to seek fullness only in Jesus! He is very clear about the priority of our love and loyalty to him, even above our family relationships.

> *Do not think that I have come to bring peace to the earth.*
> *I have not come to bring peace, but a sword.*
> *For I have come to set a man against his father,*
> *and a daughter against her mother,*
> *and a daughter-in-law against her mother-in-law.*
> *And a person's enemies will be those of his own household.*
> *Whoever loves father or mother more than me is not worthy of me,*
> *and whoever loves son or daughter more than me is not worthy of me.*
> Matthew 10:34–37

We must repent of loving others more than Christ. This is idolatry. We cannot look for our meaning and satisfaction in another person, even our spouse, and we should not want our spouse to look to us for such fulfillment either.

> All of our personal struggles come from not being full in Christ.

Certainly there is pleasure and joy in marriage. But this comes from sharing the love of Christ with one another. Marriage is the first and most important relationship in which we can fulfill our mission of helping others follow Christ. Our goal is not to make our spouses happy but to make them holy. To be holy is to be set apart for the purpose of God, and this, of course, will make a spouse truly happy. There is amazing joy in following Christ together with your husband or wife.

So our first responsibility in marriage is to find our purpose and satisfaction in Christ alone. When we do not do this, we will have problems in our marriages. That is why I often say that we don't really have "marriage problems"; we just have people problems. All of our personal struggles come from our failure to find our fullness in Christ. As James explains, we fight because of unfulfilled desires, and our desires are not fulfilled because we are not looking in the right direction (James 4:1–7).

We often think that we will fix our marriages by learning to communicate better, pleasing our partners more, or spending more time together. These are all good ideas. But the quickest way to fix your marriage is to get right with God and to rely on him alone for all your needs. Those other strategies will not be successful if the marriage is still made up of two prideful, selfish people. However, when two people are full in Christ, they are in a wonderful position to minister to each other. Then, as they minister to each other, they are able to experience the joy and intimacy that come from sharing the love of Christ.

Submission in Marriage

When a married couple can minister to each other out of fullness in Christ, they are then in a position to accomplish their purpose and mission together: to love God, love people, and make disciples. God puts husbands and wives together so that they can help each other fulfill this mission. A married couple is a ministry team. As a ministry team, it is important for them to function well together. As we have discussed already, this functionality will come through mutual submission. First, a husband and wife submit to one another in *love* by placing the other's

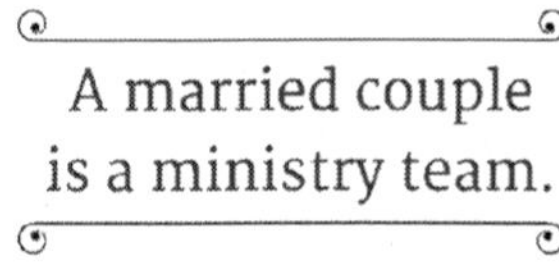
A married couple
is a ministry team.

needs before his or her own. We have already talked about how a married couple can love each other in this way. Now, let's talk some more about the other reasons we submit to one another: *truth* and *authority*. These forms of submission are critical to having a marriage that works.

A couple can learn to submit to one another in *truth* because a Christian marriage is one in which Jesus is Lord. Jesus rules by the revelation of his Word and the presence of his Spirit in our lives. A couple that wants to bring honor to Christ and to have unity in his mission will be mutually submitted to the truth of his Word and the leading of his Spirit. Because of this commitment, the husband and the wife will also submit to each other in truth. Each one is responsible to speak truth to the other in love, and each one is responsible to submit to any truth spoken.

The final form of submission that applies in the marriage is submission to *authority*. God has given the husband the responsibility to love and care for his wife. He has also given him the authority to lead in the marriage, and he calls the wife to submit to the husband's leadership (Eph. 5:22–33; Col. 3:18; 1 Pet. 3:1–6).

This is yet another way that the culture has denied God's design for marriage. Our culture generally refuses to acknowledge the leadership of the husband. We are taught that if men and women are to be thought of as equal, then one must not lead the other. However, having identical roles and responsibilities is not the same as being equal in value and dignity. Men and women are equal in dignity and value before the Lord and should be treated accordingly. At the same time, they have different roles and responsibilities.

God has authorized the husband to lead with self-sacrificial love and care in obedience to Christ. If the husband chooses to lead with a selfish agenda, then he is abusing his position and not operating in the authority Christ has given to him. A wife is called to submit to her husband "as to the Lord" (Eph. 5:22). This means that her choice to submit to her husband is in fact a choice to submit to God. Her husband will not always be right in his leadership, but even when he makes mistakes, she can rest in the love and protection of God, to whom she is ultimately submitting. Wives are even called to submit to husbands who do not obey the Word (1 Pet. 3:1–2)! However, she is not called to submit to leadership that requires disobedience to God.

There is so much more to discuss about marriage that we can't cover here. Gary Thomas's book on marriage (*Sacred Marriage: What If God Designed Marriage to Make Us Holy More Than to Make Us Happy?*) is a great resource for further study.

Parenting

The last time my mom tried to spank me, I was just about as big as she was. Of course, my mother is a pretty small lady! As she approached me in the hallway with the spanking utensil, I reasoned with her. "Mom, can't we talk about this?"

"No!" was her answer, and she just kept coming.

I continued to try to talk with her about it, but she had no intentions of talking. Finally, I reached out and took the paddle from her! I shudder to think what would have happened if my dad had been home at the time.

My mom thought I needed discipline, but I figured we could just talk. This story serves to illustrate the difficulty of parenting a child who is old enough to disciple but still may need discipline. When is it time for discipline, and when is it time for discipleship?

God gives parents, particularly fathers, the responsibility to both discipline and disciple their children.

Fathers, do not provoke your children to anger,
but bring them up in the discipline and instruction of the Lord.
Ephesians 6:4

Let's look at these two areas in turn and then see how they relate to each other.

Discipline

First, parents have authority to discipline their children (see Prov. 13:24, 22:15, 23:14, 29:17; Heb. 12:7–11). Discipline is the use of external motivation to train behavior. It can take various forms of negative consequences for wrong behavior. One that is clearly described in Scripture, but which our culture generally no longer approves of, is spanking. There are also positive ways of encouraging good behavior through affirmation and rewards.

Here are a few basic tips for effective discipline:

- Train your children to look you in the eye when you speak to them.
- Train your children to respond respectfully to your instructions with "Yes, sir" or "Yes, ma'am."
- Train your children to obey the first time. Your children will learn when you expect them to obey. If you count to three, they will wait until *two.* If you count to ten, they will often wait until you count *nine.* If you don't discipline your children until after you yell at them, then they will not obey you until you yell at them. But if you lovingly, calmly, and consistently discipline your child the first time he or she disobeys, your child will learn to listen the first time you give an instruction.
- Never spank or discipline out of anger or in such a way that would cause harm to your child.
- Hold your child responsible only for what he or she understands.
- Be creative with ways of giving your children consequences for disobedience and disrespect. When possible, give consequences that relate to the area of disobedience.
- Remember that children are different and that some forms of discipline will be much more effective on some than others. Find out what best gets your child's attention.

Discipleship

The next and most important responsibility parents have is discipleship. When Jesus answered the question about the most important commandment of all, he quoted from Deuteronomy 6:4. Look at what Moses said right after this most important commandment:

You shall love the LORD your God with all your heart
and with all your soul and with all your might.
And these words that I command you today shall be on your heart.

You shall teach them diligently to your children,
and shall talk of them when you sit in your house, and when you walk by the way,
and when you lie down, and when you rise.
Deuteronomy 6:5–7

The ultimate goal for parents is to raise mature, Christ-loving believers. This fits into God's mission for us to help others to love God and follow Jesus.

> The primary responsibility of discipleship belongs to parents.

Another way that our American culture has eroded the strength of the family is by encouraging parents to abdicate to others the responsibility of teaching their children. Many parents feel it is the church's job to disciple their children. They depend on the pastor, the Sunday School teacher, and the children's or youth pastor to teach their children about God. Pastors, and the rest of the body of Christ, are certainly responsible for discipleship. But the primary responsibility of discipleship belongs to parents.

Many parents are also realizing that they are capable of facilitating the education of their children. They have discovered the moral, spiritual, social, and academic benefits of teaching their children at home. Parents can seek the Lord for direction for their family on this important topic. Make sure that your decision is not based on what you think you are capable of, what you can afford, or what others will think of you. These are not substantial reasons by which to decide what is best for your child. God can provide for you and empower you to do whatever he calls you to do.

Some parents don't feel equipped to disciple their children. That is what this book is for! This is a practical handbook for discipleship. I have included what I consider to be the most important basic truths and practices for introducing people to Christ and helping them learn to love and follow God.

Transitioning from Discipline to Discipleship

When my children turn eight, I bring them into my office and explain to them that it is time to turn their lives over to Christ. I explain the Gospel to them and then tell them to pray to receive Christ, or I am going to spank them.

No need to read that paragraph again. You know that that would be ridiculous, because faith and a real relationship with Christ are based on the free choice of the individual. This reflection helps us understand how different the parental responsibilities of discipline and discipleship are. As we have noted, discipline uses external motivation to bring about a change in behavior. Discipleship is leading by example and guiding children toward freely giving their hearts to Jesus.

As I mentioned before, one of the most confusing times in parenting is when the children should be transitioning out of discipline and into discipleship. Parents need to discern when to move from discipline to discipleship, from external motivation to internal motivation (Prov. 13:24, 23:26). This chart helps explain the process. The chart moves from left to right, following the age of a child, from birth to adulthood.[13]

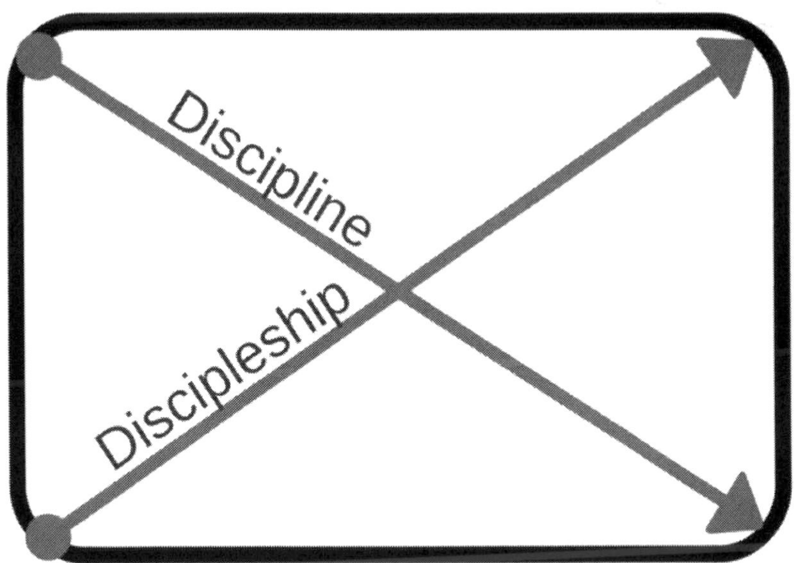

Both discipline and discipleship may take place throughout the time your children are in your home. But when a child is very young, parents exercise maximum control (or discipline) in the child's life. This is when behavior training begins. At this time, there is a lot of discipline and not as much discipleship taking place. Then as the child grows, he or she develops his or her own ability to respond to God. The child can choose to obey the parents willingly, because it is the right thing to do, and not just because he or she fears the consequences. The child can take care of his or her own stuff and get along with siblings out of a heart of obedience to God.

The cross point on the chart generally occurs around ages twelve to fourteen, depending on the development of the child. As you relate to your teenage children, your desire is primarily to teach them, appealing to their own consciences and desires to obey God. While discipline is based on power (the ability to carry out consequences), discipleship is based on influence, which is built on relationship. This is why it is so important to build strong, open relationships with your children.

Parents often experience a great deal of frustration and confusion at the cross point. *When should I discipline, and when should I disciple?* Here is a biblical principle to help guide you: give correction in the form of discipleship instead of discipline when there is respect and teachability (Ps. 25:8–15, 32:8–9). When you begin to correct your child, you can set out this choice before him or her: "If you will listen to me respectfully and receive correction, then I will teach you and help you grow. If you will not, then I will continue to discipline you until you are teachable."

Discipleship is based on influence, which is built on relationship.

Here are a few other ways you can help your children develop self-motivation based on faith in Christ.

- Pray for your children to surrender their hearts to Christ (Eph. 3:14–21).
- Teach your children truth from God's Word (Ps. 19:7–11).

- Teach your children God's purpose for life and how everything we do fits into it (Deut. 6:4–9).
- Encourage and affirm your children (1 Thess. 2:11–12).
- Offer new responsibility and freedom in response to obedience and respect (Matt. 25:14–30).
- Give your children freedom to make their own choices so that they can develop conviction (Heb. 5:14).
- Help your children discover their gifts, talents, and interests. Equip and free your children to purse them (Eph. 4:7, 11–12).

Children

If you are still at home under your parents' authority and you are old enough to read this book, then your responsibility ought to be clear by now. Just as a wife can submit to her husband "as to the Lord," so children can submit to their parents "in the Lord." It is an act of faith and obedience to God.

Children, obey your parents in the Lord, for this is right.
"Honor your father and mother"
(this is the first commandment with a promise),
"that it may go well with you and that you may live long in the land."
Ephesians 6:1–3

Once again, our culture has lied to us on this point. We are told that our goal is to be independent and pursue our own personal dreams and goals. You can see by now that this is not God's design for life. He intends for us always to be living in community, whether that is family, church, or society at large. As believers, we are called to live our lives always in awareness and consideration of others. We are called throughout life to submit to those whom God has placed in authority over us.

So you don't have to be like many young people, struggling and striving to be free from parents and family. Your family is exactly where God wants you to be right now. God has given you parents as your mentors and teachers. You can enjoy God's direction and protection through their leadership. Your family is a community in which you can grow and thrive, not a place to be held down. You might as well learn to live in community and submission now; you will have to live in cooperation with others and submission to authority for the rest of your life!

Discussion Questions

- What is the key to functioning well in any community or relationship?
- What are three reasons we ought to submit to one another?
- If you are not married, what should your attitude be about being married?
- What does our culture say about marriage that is different than what God says?
- What is one of the biggest mistakes that people make about the purpose of marriage?
- What is our first responsibility in marriage?
- What authority structure has God built into marriage?
- What two responsibilities has God given to parents?
- What is the ultimate goal of parenting?
- How can parents know when to discipline and when to disciple their children?
- What kind of attitude should a young person have toward family and authority?

Big Ideas

- God does not intend for us to operate independently.
- Learning to love God includes learning how he wants us to function and to accomplish his mission in various communities.

- Submission is the key to functioning well in any community or relationship.
- The Bible reveals at least three important reasons we ought to submit to one another:
    - Love: We submit to each other because we want what is best for each other.
    - Truth: We submit to one another when we speak what is true and right to each other.
    - Authority: We submit to those to whom God has given the responsibility to lead.
- God says that marriage is good and necessary for most people (Gen. 2:18, 24).
- God says that sexual intimacy should take place only within the context of a marriage between one woman and one man, who are married for life (Matt. 19:4–5; Eph. 5:3; Heb. 13:4).
- Our goal is not to make our spouses happy but to make them holy, which means to be set apart for the purpose of God.
- Our first responsibility in marriage is to find our purpose and satisfaction in Christ alone.
- God puts a husband and wife together so that they can help each other fulfill God's mission. A married couple is a ministry team.
- A couple that wants to bring honor to Christ and to have unity in his mission will be mutually submitted to the truth of his Word and the leading of his Spirit.
- God has given the husband the responsibility to love and care for his wife. He has also given him the authority to lead in the marriage and calls the wife to submit to his leadership (Eph. 5:22–33).
- God gives parents, particularly fathers, the responsibility to discipline and disciple their children.
- The ultimate goal for parents is to raise mature, Christ-loving believers. Generally, parenting should move from discipline to discipleship, from external motivation to internal motivation (Prov. 13:24, 23:26).

- Give correction in the form of discipleship instead of discipline when there is respect and teachability (Ps. 25:8–15, 32:8–9).
- Children can submit to their parents "in the Lord" as an act of faith and obedience to God.

For Further Reading

Thomas, Gary. 2000. *Sacred Marriage: What If God Designed Marriage to Make Us Holy More Than to Make Us Happy?* Grand Rapids: Zondervan.

Tripp, Ted. 2005. *Shepherding a Child's Heart*, 2nd ed. Wapwallopen, PA: Shepherd Press.

CHAPTER 11

Living in Community—Church

—∾—

"Going to church doesn't make you a Christian any more than going to McDonald's makes you a hamburger." As a young boy, I grew up listening to Keith Green, and I always loved this line. He stated this in a live recorded concert as he introduced one of his songs.

While this statement is certainly true, I have often heard it used as a reason why Christians do not have to go to church! "Besides," some say, "I can worship God better out in creation, like on the golf course or lake." Since going to church doesn't save you, is it optional for the Christian life?

God has created us to live in community with others. In addition to marriage and our family relationships, he has placed us in community with his people—the church. In this chapter, we will continue to explore biblical principles related to living in community, and we will discuss our place in the church and how to resolve conflict with others.

Church

The word *church* in the Bible refers to a gathering or a community of people. When talking about the Christian church, the Bible refers to the *gathering* of believers (Matt. 18:17; 1 Cor. 11:18), the *local community* of believers (Phil. 4:15), or the *global body* of believers (Eph. 1:22). The Bible never refers to a building as a church because believers in Jesus Christ *are* the church. The church is God's family. He is our Father, and we are brothers and sisters in Christ (Matt. 23:8–9). Being a part of the life of a local church is important because it provides the ongoing personal relationships necessary for New Testament Christian living.

And let us consider how to stir up one another to love and good works, not neglecting to meet together, as is the habit of some, but encouraging one another, and all the more as you see the Day drawing near.
Hebrews 10:24–25

Let's briefly explore eight ways the local church follows Christ together.

1. *The local church gathers together each week* (Heb. 10:24–25; Acts 20:7; 1 Cor. 16:1–2). These days, there are many ways to be connected with others that do not include meeting them in person. We can talk on the phone, text, e-mail, video chat, and follow each other on social media. We can even watch church on television! Because of this, some Christians do not think that meeting together with God's people each week is important. However, nothing can replace the real, personal interactions we share when believers meet together. The rest of this list includes some of the important things that the local church does together when it meets.
2. *The local church worships together* (Acts 2:42; 2 Tim. 2:8; 1 Cor. 14:26; Matt. 18:19–20). Just about everything a church does together can be considered worship, but I am particularly talking about worship through music and prayer. As we have already discussed, worship and prayer are an important part of the individual believer's life, but God also calls us to corporate worship. I hope you have experienced the powerful encouragement and transformation that comes from worshiping with God's people!
3. *The local church ministers to each other through spiritual gifts* (1 Cor. 14:19, 23, 26, 28; Eph. 4:11–16). We can use our spiritual gifts each day to minister to others, but it is a unique time of ministry when all the members of a local church gather for worship. When Paul teaches about spiritual gifts in 1 Corinthians 14, he is giving instructions on how believers are to minister to one another when "the whole church comes together" (v. 23).
4. *The local church partakes of the Lord's Supper together* (1 Cor. 10:17, 11:17–34). I have heard of people taking the Lord's Supper by themselves. I

suppose there is nothing wrong with that, but the assumption in Scripture is that the local church takes the Lord's Supper when they gather together. In the early church, it was part of a fellowship meal. The Bible teaches that the Lord's Supper represents not just what Christ has done for us on the cross, but our unity and fellowship with one another.

> *Because there is one bread, we who are many are one body,*
> *for we all partake of the one bread.*
> 1 Corinthians 10:17

5. *The local church learns from God's Word together* (Acts 2:42; 1 Tim. 4:6, 13; 2 Tim. 4:1–5). In the New Testament, the teaching of God's Word is one of the most important aspects of the gathering of the local church. Today, we have the unprecedented opportunity to listen to great Bible teachers from all over the world through radio, television, and the Internet. This is a great treasure! However, Bible teaching in the local church plays a unique role in the believer's life that cannot be replaced. For example, in the Bible, we see the church having spontaneous dialogue and discussion when it meets (especially in Acts and 1 Corinthians). In our church, we have what we call "open time" after the sermon. During this time, the church has the opportunity to ask the teacher questions or offer comments. Others can teach, prophesy, testify, and discuss issues of doctrine and practice. Larger churches may have small-group Bible studies, so these kinds of discussions can take place there.
6. *The local church has designated leadership* (Acts 20:28–30; Titus 1:5; 1 Tim. 5:17–21). According to the New Testament, each local church has elders (pastors) and deacons to lead and serve them. Deacons are responsible for serving the practical needs of a congregation, while pastors are responsible for teaching, leading, and caring for their spiritual needs. The local church plays an important role in observing the qualifications of pastors and deacons, appointing them to their positions, and confronting them for sin.
7. *The local church holds itself accountable for righteousness* (1 Cor. 5:4; Matt. 18:15–20). There are many passages that instruct Christians to

warn, correct, and rebuke each other. God wants us to help each other live lives that are pleasing to the Lord. We can do this with all believers, but the local church has a particular responsibility to keep itself pure. It is the local church that is responsible for holding its members accountable for unrepentant sin. Unfortunately, many churches today do not take this responsibility seriously. First, church meetings are often structured in such a way that it is easy for a believer to come in, attend the service, and go home without really getting to know anyone. Second, many believers regularly move from church to church and therefore avoid being known or held accountable for their behavior. Finally, many churches are simply unwilling to deal with sin. In the next section on biblical conflict resolution, we will discuss in depth how to communicate with others when we are concerned that they are headed in the wrong directions.

The most important basis for unity in the church is the Gospel.

8. *The local church works together to make disciples* (Phil. 1:27–30). Making disciples is not only our mission as individual believers, it is also the mission of the church. Local churches can pray, send missionaries, collect resources, evangelize their own regions, and work with other churches to provide support and further the Gospel. The most important basis for unity in the church is the Gospel. This is faith in the substitutionary atonement for our sin through the death and resurrection of Jesus Christ. Our unity is based on other important doctrines as well. The deity of Christ and the doctrine of the Trinity separate the true church of Christ from false churches or cults. There is so much to talk about when it comes to the importance and biblical teaching of the church. The main point here is that it is important for each believer to be a part of a local church. Look for a church that clearly proclaims the Gospel, believes in the authority of Scripture, teaches the Bible faithfully, and is committed to making disciples.

Biblical Conflict Resolution

As you probably know, when you choose to be part of a local church, you are going to have to relate to difficult people. We can enjoy the fellowship, love, and cooperation we share with our family and friends, but there is also frustration and pain! We often do not agree. We hurt or get hurt by others. When we act wrongly, it affects those around us.

What should we do when we are hurt or believe that those around us are doing something wrong? What should we do when we think that those we love are headed for trouble? How do we help them? God tells us how to handle these things in his Word. Let me suggest the following nine steps you can take (and retake) when you face these difficulties in your relationships.

1. *Give space.* When Dana and I were first married, I asked my older brother Michael to give me some marriage advice. He said, "One of the most important lessons I have learned in marriage is that I am not my wife's Holy Spirit, and she isn't mine."

This was good advice because most of us have a tendency to try to fix the people in our lives. When we see something we think is wrong, it is easy to jump right in and try to make it right. While we certainly have a responsibility to try to help others live lives that are pleasing to the Lord, we must also remember that God is the only one who can really change people. Often, by trying to fix others, we become obstacles to their learning processes. This is why I suggest that our first response when we see problems in others' lives is to give time and space for God to work.

There is another reason we should not immediately try to correct others when we have a conflict. Some of us tend to speak before we think, or we become easily angered. James advises:

> God is the only one who can really change people.

Be quick to hear, slow to speak, slow to anger.
James 1:19

So the first thing I am going to do when I think someone else is wrong about something is nothing. With humility and patience, I will give the other person space to make mistakes and learn from them.

You may be thinking, *But I can't do nothing! This is too important!* Don't forget that this is only the first step. The second step provides another great reason we should not dive right into correcting others.

2. *Check yourself.* Jesus has given us some helpful advice when we are trying to help others with their problems.

Why do you see the speck that is in your brother's eye,
but do not notice the log that is in your own eye?
Or how can you say to your brother, "Let me take the speck out of your eye,"
when there is the log in your own eye?
You hypocrite, first take the log out of your own eye,
and then you will see clearly to take the speck out of your brother's eye.
Matthew 7:3–5

It is easier to see that someone else is wrong than to detect our own mistakes. So when I am in conflict with others and I choose to give space and check myself, I often find that the main problem is actually me! *Checking myself* means that I get alone with God and ask him to convict me of sin and help me to understand the situation better.

Jesus says that when I have discerned, confessed, and requested forgiveness for any wrongdoing on my part, I am in a better position to help others. In fact, asking for forgiveness often clears up the waters for others to see their own issues. It also strengthens the relationship and clears the way to address those issues when the time is right. If we will follow Jesus's instruction, we will be sure not to go to others about their sins when there is still unconfessed sin on our part in the relationship.

3. *Let go of anger.* When we are hurt by others or think that what they are doing is wrong, we often become angry. This is another reason we

might want to stop and reflect before we try to correct others. Trying to have a discussion when we are angry rarely produces good results! More importantly, Paul warns us that allowing anger to settle into our hearts is spiritually dangerous (Eph. 4:26–27). The way that God wants us to deal with our anger is by learning to forgive others. Failure to forgive is a sin and therefore becomes an obstacle in one's relationship with God (Matt. 6:14–15).

Forgiveness takes place at two levels. One is on the relational level, where we extend forgiveness to a repentant person and the relationship is restored. Another is on the heart level. Even if someone does not repent, we must not be resentful or hold onto anger. We can forgive the person in our heart, even if the relationship has not yet been restored. This heart-level forgiveness is how we let go of anger. We *can* and *must* forgive because we have been forgiven (Matt. 18:21–35).

4. *Love.* Sometimes when we are in conflict with someone, we withdrawal from him or her. This is usually an attempt to protect ourselves or to influence the other person by expressing our disapproval of them. I can remember times that I chose not to hold Dana's hand or show affection because I was upset with her about something. I am embarrassed to admit this, even though I'm pretty sure you have done it, too. This is not how love behaves. Instead, love is when we do what is best for someone else, even when it costs us. Love does not choose its course of action based on personal hurt and loss. Jesus says, "Love your enemies and pray for those who persecute you" (Matt. 5:44). This demonstrates that, although we are hurt and our relationships are broken, we can still love.

So how does love behave? Paul describes it to us:

> *Love is patient and kind; love does not envy or boast;*
> *it is not arrogant or rude. It does not insist on its own way;*
> *it is not irritable or resentful.*
> 1 Corinthians 13:4–5

> Even when we are hurt and our relationships are broken, we can love.

Even when we are in conflict with others, we are able to follow love instead of lashing out or pulling back.

This step in the process means that you choose to reach out and express love and affirmation, even when things are not resolved. This will solidify your forgiveness and strengthen your relational foundation so that you can deal with difficult subjects at the right time.

5. *Pray.* As we have already pointed out, we are not really able to change others. Who can change them? Jesus can. So it makes sense to talk to *him* about the situation. We can pray for the work of the Spirit to convict the other person if we believe he is wrong about something. We can pray about how and when to bring up the matter with him. Allow God to lead you in handling the situation. As you seek him, the Lord may even tell you to wait patiently and let him handle the situation (Matt. 5:44; James 1:5–8).

6. *Talk.* At this point in the nine steps to biblical resolution, we finally get to do what we've been chomping at the bit to do since the problem first began: *talk about it.* Hopefully, taking the other steps first has prevented us from making some major mistakes. If we have made it this far in the process and still believe that there is a legitimate issue that needs to be resolved, then it is time to talk about it. However, let's pay close attention to the way God teaches us to handle such things.

First, *ask questions.* We should not come into the conversation with guns blazing, firing off our accusations. Here is a wise saying:

If one gives an answer before he hears, it is his folly and shame.
Proverbs 18:13

Bring up the topic by asking for more information about what happened, how the other person feels about it, or what motivated his or her behavior. *Listen*, and try to understand what he or she says.

Second, *be gentle and kind.* Even if we are asking questions, we are probably poking into a sensitive area. Here is another wise word:

A soft answer turns away wrath, but a harsh word stirs up anger.
Proverbs 15:1

When we approach people with accusations or harshness, then they immediately are put on the defense. When we approach them with openness and gentleness, we give them space to own their own mistakes without having to confront them.

7. *Discern the issue.* Now that you have asked questions and gained more information, the next task in the conversation is to discern what kind of issue you are facing. I will suggest two basic categories:

a. Issues of a secondary nature, involving personal conviction or preference
b. Issues involving violations of biblical principle

Many people seem more willing to argue about how to load the dishwasher or how to organize church projects than to deal with issues that really matter. Paul warns the Romans "not to quarrel over opinions" (Rom. 14:1). On these secondary issues, "each one should be fully convinced in his own mind" (Rom. 14:5). We can certainly discuss questions of opinion or the best way to get something done, but we must do so with humility and patience. Ultimately, we must be willing to let it go and let the other person live according to his or her own conviction.

By going through these steps, we may discover that many of our problems with others are not legitimate issues at all. However, if you believe that you are dealing with an issue involving the violation of a biblical principle, then it is time to move to step 8.

8. *Speak the truth.* Jesus has given us the responsibility of going to our brother in the Lord and confronting him for his sin (Matt. 18:15). We don't do this because of how his sin affects us or to get an apology. We confront him for his own good so that he can repent and avoid the harm that comes from sin

(James 1:15). How we handle this is important. Paul explains that we are to speak the truth in love (Eph. 4:15) and "restore him in a spirit of gentleness" (Gal. 6:1). So with a spirit of love and gentleness, we appeal to our brother to repent of his sin. We have to put aside our fear of offending the other person or putting strain on our friendship. It is much more important to help people turn to God than to make sure everyone stays comfortable!

9. *Give space.* Now we are back to the first step. Once you have spoken truth, give the other person time to process it. Unless you sense that he or she is ready to repent, you might want to end the conversation with this question: "Will you please pray about and consider what I have said?"

How long does it take to go through all these steps? There is no set amount of time that they will require. We must walk through them, depending on the Lord for wisdom and leadership. We should be willing for it to take much longer than we want it to. But that doesn't mean it will. Many of these are basic issues of Christian maturity. When we incorporate these behaviors into our everyday lives, we may be able to process a conflict almost immediately.

Discussion Questions

- Why is it important to be a part of a local church?
- What are some of the things that a local church does when it meets together?
- Which steps for biblical conflict resolution are most difficult for you?

Big Ideas

- Believers in Jesus Christ *are* the church.
- There are eight ways the local church follows Christ together:
    - The local church gathers together each week.
    - The local church worships together.
    - The local church ministers to each other through spiritual gifts.

- The local church partakes of the Lord's Supper together.
- The local church learns from God's Word together.
- The local church has designated leadership.
- The local church holds itself accountable for righteousness.
- The local church works together to make disciples.

- There are nine steps you can take (and retake) when you face difficulties in your relationships.
    - Give space.
    - Check yourself.
    - Let go of anger.
    - Love.
    - Pray.
    - Talk about it.
    - Discern the issue.
    - Speak the truth.
    - Give space.

CHAPTER 12

Discerning God's Will

—~~—

A FRIEND OF MINE RECENTLY told me that God led him to move to another country...again. This wasn't the first time. In fact, several other times, he told me he was moving to another country. The problem was that he has never moved anywhere.

I have met many others who told me that God led them to take this job or marry that person. But after things didn't quite work out like they expected, they decided to take a new direction. After experiences like these, many believers find themselves confused and disillusioned when trying to understand and follow God's will. Did they not really hear from God? Or did they simply not follow through on what God had said when the going got tough?

If you ask a Christian whether he or she would like to know God's will for his or her life, the person will likely say, "Yes, I would love to know God's will for my life!"

If you ask the person, "Do you know how to find out God's will for your life?" he or she may pause and think. "Hmm...I'm not sure."

I have met many believers who do not have confidence that they can discern God's leading in their lives. I have also met believers who have plenty of confidence but probably shouldn't. In other words, they are operating on questionable understandings of how to discern God's will. In some ways, God's will and purposes will be accomplished no matter what we do. God "works all things according to the counsel of his will" (Eph. 1:11). The creation of the universe and God's provision for salvation in Jesus Christ were parts of God's unalterable plans (Rev. 4:11; Gal. 1:4). Also, no matter what we do, Jesus Christ is going to return, judge the world, and raise those who trust in him to eternal life (John 6:39–40; Eph. 1:7–10).

In other ways, the will of God is either carried out or not carried out in people's lives. As we have already discussed, sin is the rejection of God and his will. That is why doing God's will is a characteristic of believers (Matt. 7:21, 12:50, 25:31–46). We are exhorted in Scripture to make an effort to discern, understand, and live out God's will (Rom. 12:2; 1 Pet. 4:2; Heb. 10:36).

Try to discern what is pleasing to the Lord…
Therefore do not be foolish, but understand what the will of the Lord is.
Ephesians 5:10, 17

Paul says it is foolish not to know and do God's will! This is because we know that God is wise, trustworthy, and loving (Num. 23:19; Isa. 40:13–14). We know that God's will is good for us (Jer. 29:11; Rom. 12:2) and that we need his help because we are not wise on our own (James 1:5–8; Prov. 3:5–8).

We will devote the rest of this chapter to exploring nine important principles for understanding God's will for our lives. These are separated into five *foundations* for discerning God's will and four *avenues* for discerning God's will. For further study, you may want to take the time to read the passages that are listed after each principle.

Five Foundations for Discerning God's Will

1. *We can discern God's will by surrendering our lives to him* (Rom. 12:1–2; John 4:34; 5:30, 39–40; 6:38; 7:16–17; Luke 9:23–25).

   When I was a camp counselor one summer, a young camper named Julie approached me with a question. She expressed concern that God had not been speaking to her recently and wondered what might be wrong. With unexpected wisdom, I asked her, "Do you remember the last time God spoke to you?"

   After reflecting for a moment, she said, "Yes."

   "What did you do in response to what God said?"

She stood there looking at me as she processed that question. Then, a look of realization and conviction crept across her face. I didn't have to say anything else.

If we are ignoring what God has already told us in his Word or convicted us of by his Spirit, then we are not in a good position to receive further leading from the Lord. Jesus explains to whom he reveals himself:

Whoever has my commandments and keeps them, he it is who loves me.
And he who loves me will be loved by my Father,
and I will love him and manifest myself to him.
John 14:21

Sometimes when I get into a difficult situation and go to God to get some help and direction, I sense that he is saying to me, "Good! I am glad you are here. There are some things I have been wanting to talk with you about." When we need direction from the Lord, a great place to start is to work through the "Getting Right with God" section of this book (chapter 2). Before we seek the Lord for answers or direction on a particular topic, we want to make sure we take a place of complete surrender before him. Are we walking in obedience to Christ to the best of our ability and knowledge up to this point?

Another important aspect of surrendering our lives to Christ is to have a simple willingness to do whatever he wants us to do. I remember when my best friend in high school was struggling with a call from God. He confessed to me that he would do whatever God wanted him to do…except be a pastor. My friend was not in a position to hear from God, was he? But he got down on his knees, and praying and weeping, he let go of his fears and desires and surrendered unconditionally to God's call.

I also remember desperately calling out to God to know his will about whether I should marry a particular young lady. I struggled to get peace and clarity. In retrospect, I can see that I was struggling with my own desires and agenda. Instead of really wanting to hear

God's will, I wanted him to confirm my own will!

"Lord, I want to do whatever you want me to."

If you are having trouble surrendering to God's will, try praying this prayer. "Lord, I want to do whatever you want me to. Whatever! I deny myself and renounce my own desires and dreams, trusting that your eternal wisdom and love are better. On this particular issue, I only want to know what will please you most."

2. *We can discern God's will by studying Scripture* (Ps. 19:7–11; 1 Thess. 4:1–6; 2 Tim. 3:16–17).

   We have already discussed the importance of Scripture in the believer's life. We have described how we can pray, meditate on, read, and study God's Word. The more we understand Scripture and have his wisdom, the clearer the right paths will become for us (Heb. 5:11–14). Paul has this to say about discerning God's will:

Do not be conformed to this world, but be transformed by the renewal of your mind,
that by testing you may discern what is the will of God,
what is good and acceptable and perfect.
Romans 12:2

How are our minds renewed? How are our thoughts and attitudes changed? We learn from the psalmist that we are changed by God's Word.

The law of the LORD is perfect, reviving the soul;
the testimony of the LORD is sure, making wise the simple;
the precepts of the LORD are right, rejoicing the heart;
the commandment of the LORD is pure, enlightening the eyes;
Psalm 19:7–8

If we want to know God's will, then our first task ought to be to discover what he has already revealed about his will in Scripture. God has already revealed to us that he wants us to love him, love people, and make disciples. He has also shown us many specific ways that he wants us to do these things. Many believers are seeking God's will on something when they really just need to get busy doing what God has already revealed in his Word.

If we are seeking his direction about a matter that is not specifically addressed in Scripture, we can be sure that he will lead us in a way that is consistent with what he has already revealed. The Bible is authoritative in the believer's life, so anything that we believe to be true and right should be tested by Scripture (Acts 17:11; 1 John 4:1–6; Titus 1:9).

3. *We can discern God's will by seeking him in prayer* (Phil. 4:6–7; Jer. 29:11–13; James 4:2b).

   God loves for us to seek him and his will in prayer. When we ask for anything according to his will, he hears and answers us (1 John 5:14–15). So here is a simple question: Does God want us to know and do his will? Of course! We can have absolute confidence and peace that God will direct us as we seek him.

   I meet believers who are afraid that they are going to miss God's will. They worry that God is trying to speak to them, but they just can't hear it. However, God is not playing games with us. He is not leaving hints to a puzzle we must figure out. He knows what we know, and he is able to communicate with us. We can have the confidence and peacefulness of a child who knows that his Heavenly Father can handle it! If we are stressed and afraid as we seek God, then we are not trusting that he is able and willing to show us his will.

4. *We can discern God's will by waiting for him to lead us* (Ps. 25:4–5, 106:13).

   If we have confidence that God wants to show us his will, then we will be able to *wait* on him to lead us. Since God's timing is rarely our timing, we often get impatient and are tempted jump ahead of God. We sense the pressure of a decision we have to make or the urgency of a problem we need to solve. But many times, the pressure and urgency we sense about an issue are only apparent. Problems often disappear, or two choices turn into three or none. When we wait on God, he often opens up new opportunities that were not yet available to us. It is easy to jump at something good before we have even discovered what is best.

As we learn to wait on the Lord, we should remember that waiting doesn't mean sitting around. Instead, we are to keep busy with what God has already given us to do. In addition, seeking God is quite active. We pray, study Scripture, observe our desires and abilities, ask for advice, think, conduct diligent research, and observe his work in our circumstances.

As I have sought the Lord over the years, I have learned what it feels like to be pushing ahead on something instead of letting it unfold in God's timing. There is a different kind of peace and certainty when it unfolds in God's timing. Be patient, and wait until you are certain that God is leading you. If we take action without understanding God's will, then we are not acting in faith, and "whatever does not proceed from faith is sin" (Rom. 14:23).

5. *We can discern God's will by listening to the testimony of the Holy Spirit.*

   The Spirit has a ministry of witnessing to the truth (Acts 5:32, 20:23; Rom. 8:16; John 15:26, 16:7–11). When we are walking in disobedience, God convicts us and calls us to him through his Spirit. But when we trust and walk with God, there is peace (Isa. 26:3–4; Phil. 4:6–9). Peace is much more than how we feel about something; it is a supernatural sense of rightness that comes from God.

   This sense of peace is developed from a daily walk of obedience and trust. We learn to discern the leading of the Holy Spirit as we become more immersed in God's Word and learn to walk in obedience to what he is saying to us. You can review how to recognize the leading of the Spirit in chapter 7.

Four Avenues for Discerning God's Will

1. *We can discern God's will by observing our personal desires, convictions, and abilities* (1 Cor. 7:8–9, 36–38; Exod. 25:2; 2 Thess. 3:5; 1 Cor. 12:4–7, 11).

   Although we have sinful desires that tempt us to disobey, God also gives us good desires that help direct our lives. It is not difficult to identify sinful desires (Gal. 5:19–21). Any desires that we have that are not sinful ought to be taken into consideration as we seek God's direction. We should observe the things we feel strongly about, the strengths of our personalities, and the natural talents and spiritual gifts that God has given us. All of these have been given to us by God as a part of his design for accomplishing his mission for us. Observing how God has made us is an important part of understanding his will for our lives. Now, we should not conclude that we know God's will just because we want to do something. These desires, convictions, and abilities must be understood in light of the other eight ways we can discern God's will.

2. *We can discern God's will by observing God's work in our circumstances* (James 4:13–17; 1 Kings 12:15; 1 Cor. 16:8–9; 1 Pet. 3:17; 4:19).

   God causes and allows particular circumstances to take place in order to direct our lives. This does not mean that everything that happens is God's will or is caused by God. For example, God may allow, but does not cause, the enemy to set our circumstances against us in order to deter us from doing God's will (Job 1:6–10; Eph. 6:11). And we know that temptations are not caused by God (James 1:13). This is why we can never determine God's will by circumstances alone.

   God will open and close doors as a way of leading us.

   At the same time, we know that God will open and close doors as a way of leading us. We also know that God will provide everything necessary for the completion of his will. Whatever wisdom, strength, ability, or resources we need to do what God wants us to do, he will provide. God's provisions as we obey are confirmations of his direction.

Another way we can discern God's will through our circumstances is by observing how he has worked in our lives in the past. Sometimes these are called "spiritual markers." Henry Blackaby and Claude King explain: "Each time I have encountered God's call or direction for my life, I have mentally built a spiritual marker at that point. A spiritual marker identifies a time of transition, decision, or direction when I clearly know that God has guided me...When I face a decision about God's direction...I look to see which one of the options seems to be most consistent with what God has been doing in my life."[14]

3. *We can discern God's will by listening to the counsel of the church* (Matt. 18:15–17; Heb. 13:17; 1 Cor. 12:4–20, 14:29–33; Prov. 15:22).

   We have already talked about the importance of living in community and submitting to the authority that God has placed in our lives. So when you are seeking God's will on a particular matter, go to those who have authority in your life and ask for their counsel. It is also helpful to get feedback from others in the body of Christ. Take the time and effort to find godly people you trust, and ask them for counsel as well. This might not be easy, because it takes humility to ask for and listen to advice from others. But we can be sure this is a part of how God intends to give us his wisdom.

   Once again, we cannot discern God's will only by listening to the advice of others. Sometimes we may receive conflicting feedback—and sometimes even godly people are wrong. But getting counsel from others is a critical piece that must be taken seriously to see how it fits into God's overall movement in our lives.

4. *We can discern God's will by reasoning and testing* (Prov. 14:15; Rom. 12:2; 1 Cor. 1:20–21, 2:4, 4:6, 10:15; Acts 17:2, 11, 17; 1 John 4:1–6; James 3:17).

Seeking truth is more than, but not less than, using our minds (Phil. 4:7; Rom. 12:2). We tend to try to think our way out of troubles or calculate the wisest decision. This is simply not enough.

Trust in the LORD with all your heart,
and do not lean on your own understanding.
Proverbs 3:5

At the same time, it is right to use our intellect as we seek God. Although God's ways transcend our understanding, his life-transforming work is generally discerned through the mind of the believer. Furthermore, while God's ways may transcend logic, they are not illogical, chaotic, or confusing. If we build our thinking on the presuppositions of the love and power of God and the revelation of his Word, then his leading is going to make sense. So as we seek God's will, we are supposed to be reflecting, thinking, remembering, paying attention, and making wise choices. As you make decisions, try to think clearly and objectively about the situation and what you know about God and his ways.

When you are seeking God's will on a particular issue, you can use the following questions to help process these foundations and avenues for discernment.

a) Am I willing to follow God's will in this matter, even if it is not what I want to do?
b) What scriptural principles are relevant to this question? Do I need to study more on this subject?
c) Have I spent significant time in prayer seeking God about this question?
d) Have I worked through any feelings of pressure or impatience? Will I wait until I am clear about God's leading?
e) Has the Spirit convicted me of any sin related to this question? Can I sense his peace in moving in a particular direction?

f) What desires and abilities has God given me that are relevant to this question?
g) How has God worked in my circumstances to lead me concerning this issue?
h) Have I sought the counsel of godly leaders and others in my church? What do they have to say about it?
i) What are the pros and cons surrounding this question? What makes most sense from a biblical perspective?
j) Has God confirmed his leading through any particular sign or impression?

Discussion Questions

- Have you ever been confused or frustrated when trying to understand God's will?
- What is the first foundation for discerning God's will?
- Which of these foundations and avenues for discerning God's will was most helpful to you?
- Which one do you find most challenging?
- Which one would you like to study more?

Big Ideas

- There are five foundations for discerning God's will:
    - We can discern God's will by surrendering our lives to him.
    - We can discern God's will by studying Scripture.
    - We can discern God's will by seeking him in prayer.
    - We can discern God's will by waiting for him to lead us.
    - We can discern God's will by listening to the testimony of the Holy Spirit.
- There are four avenues for discerning God's will:

- We can discern God's will by observing our personal desires, convictions, and abilities.
- We can discern God's will by observing God's work in our circumstances.
- We can discern God's will by listening to the counsel of the church.
- We can discern God's will by reasoning and testing.

For Further Reading

Blackaby, Henry T. and Claude V. King. 2005. *Experiencing God: Student Edition*. Nashville: LifeWay Press.

CHAPTER 13

Living Intentionally

—෴—

We have covered a lot of material; there is so much to remember and so much to do! Hopefully, you are wondering, "How can I process all this information and make plans to incorporate it into my life?" Or maybe you are hoping that, by your reading this book, some of it will just stick. Probably not. We have not been discussing just a few minor life adjustments; we have been talking about a radical life redirection! A change of life takes intentionality and resolve.

Paul encouraged the Ephesians to live intentionally:

Look carefully then how you walk, not as unwise but as wise,
making the best use of the time, because the days are evil.
Therefore do not be foolish, but understand what the will of the Lord is.
Ephesians 5:15–17

When Daniel was thrust into a new and ungodly culture, he discovered that his godly lifestyle would be challenged:

But Daniel resolved that he would not defile himself
with the king's food, or with the wine that he drank.
Daniel 1:8a

Seeing the opposition to his goals, Daniel resolved to act in faith in a certain area of his life. Resolutions are decisions we make ahead of time, when we are thinking clearly, that help us stick to it when the going gets tough.

In this chapter, I want to give you some simple tools for living with intentionality and resolve. Living intentionally is like charting a course. You carefully select your destination and then decide how you are going to get there. When we chart a course for life, we end up using words like *purpose*, *vision*, *mission*, *passion*, *goals*, and *strategy*. Some of these words have overlapping meanings, and people use them in different ways. Let me explain how I am using these words in this chapter.

Purpose

Our purpose is the reason we exist. As we have discussed in chapters 1 and 2, everyone's purpose is the same: God has created us to love him and to love people. *Everything* else in life should serve these two purposes. This will always be our purpose, even in eternity!

Mission

While our purpose is eternal, our mission is not. A mission is something that can be completed. That's why we say, "Mission accomplished!" As we discussed in chapter 9, God has given all believers the same mission: to make disciples of all nations (Matt. 28:18–20). We will love God forever, but we only have our time here on earth to make disciples.

Do you accept this mission? Are you ready to make it the practical reality of life and not just a theoretical belief? I have to admit, I think I have spent quite a bit of my life with the mission of making disciples my theoretical belief. I know many Christians who believe in Jesus and do many good things, but when we scrape down past the surface, we find selfish agendas. They do good things that are mostly not too difficult and that give good return. It is disturbing to realize that people can live what appear to be Christian lives, but they are really living for themselves! What does it take to really follow Christ? It takes a genuine heart of compassion and personal sacrifice for the good of others.

So take an honest look at your life and motives, and identify what you are truly after. Will you resolve to make loving God the driving purpose of your life? Will you accept making disciples as your real life's mission?

Although we all share this general mission, we each have unique parts to play. Each of us has a unique set of relationships, responsibilities, and abilities that determines the specifics of our mission. As you develop your own mission, think through these aspects of your life. How do these various parts of your life fit into making disciples?

- Marriage
- Children
- Work
- Finances and possessions
- Talents and gifts
- Platforms and areas of influence
- Other relationships

As you take these into consideration, you will be able to write a disciple-making mission statement that is a unique expression of God's design and call for your life. You can also write a disciple-making mission statement for each major area of your life, such as your marriage, parenting, and work.

Passion

I remember when my college writing professor made this statement in class: "Discipline is passion!" Although I did not really understand it at the time, this declaration resonated with me, and I quickly wrote it down. Since then, I have learned that the reason we deny ourselves or make hard choices is because there is something we want more. An athlete will train every day because he wants to compete in the Olympics. Someone on a diet chooses not to eat what he or she wants in order to lose weight. A passion is more than just a desire. Without passion, we will not have the focus and strength to say no to other desires that distract from our mission. Many people do not have passion, so they simply follow their desires and feelings. I have learned from experience and observation that such a life is not fulfilling nor productive.

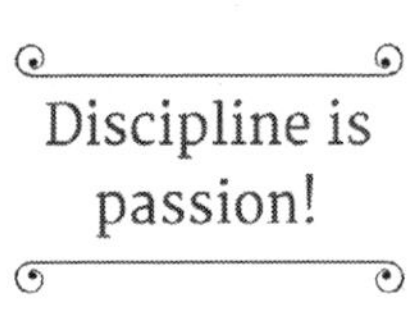

One of the ways we find our passion is to identify what is at stake. What will be the results if we fulfill our mission? What will happen if we do not fulfill our mission? For example, here is what I believe is at stake for all of us:

- *The glory of God.* God is worthy of honor and worship. My choices will bring glory to God, or they will not.
- *The souls of men.* God is using us to draw people to himself, and our efforts affect people's choices. No matter what we do, God is just, and people are responsible, but we are real players in people's eternal destinies. We must do all we can!
- *The joy of life.* So many are depressed in our generation and culture. So many have lost hope and joy. Real fulfillment and joy comes from loving and knowing God, and from serving him by loving others and making disciples. We can bring hope and joy to people by introducing them to Jesus Christ!

You can also consider what is at stake more specifically—in your marriage, your parenting, your work, and your finances. Get in touch with the reason why these things are so important. Let this understanding fuel your passion for accomplishing God's mission for your life!

Vision

A vision statement is the articulation of what it will look like when we accomplish our mission. If we have considered what is at stake, we are already on our way to getting a vision for life. We have a vision when we can identify specific outcomes of accomplishing our mission. For example, as a parent, my vision is to see my children become strong, wise, humble, loving followers of Christ who pursue God's calling for them with courage and steadfastness. I can picture each of them in this vision. This is a great source of motivation—fuel for my passion!

Goals

Once we identify our purpose, mission, passion, and vision, we are ready to chart a course for our lives. Our goals are the concrete steps we must take in order to accomplish our mission. We are able to determine our goals by looking at our destination (vision) and tracing our steps back to where we are. We set our goals by determining what will move us from where we are to the completion of our mission. Some of these are things we will be able to accomplish right away, while others must wait.

We can separate our goals into two types: *habits* and *projects*. Some of the most important goals we can set are to establish *habits* necessary for completing our mission. We have covered many such habits in this book: spending regular time with God in prayer and Bible study, memorizing Scripture, fostering family discipleship, and staying physically healthy. You will be able to identify other habits we have not discussed that will be important for accomplishing your mission. A *project* goal is a specific, measurable objective with a specific deadline (e.g., write a book by May, start a business this year, have a family over for dinner next week, and so forth).

As you develop your goals, try to keep in mind the various aspects of your life. The most important is your relationship with God. Next, consider your personal heath. As the airline flight attendant warns: "Please put on your own oxygen mask before helping others." If you have passed out from lack of oxygen, you will not be helping very many people! After you have attended to your own physical and spiritual health, you can consider your home responsibilities, work, finances, and ministry. You may end up with goals for each of these areas of life.

Strategies

Strategies are the specific steps we take and tools we use to accomplish our goals. These specific steps are called tasks. This is what we put on our to-do lists and calendars. Some people don't consistently use to-do lists or calendars. However, if we are going to live intentionally and accomplish our goals, we will have to stay organized! There are a number of books that can help you think through priorities and goals and stay organized. Two such books that I have found especially helpful are David Allen's *Getting Things Done: The Art of Stress-Free Productivity* and Stephen R. Covey's *First Things First*. You will find great ideas from these authors that you have not thought of before! Think through these and other ways to stay organized, then come up with a strategy that works for you.

The main point here is that we learn how to organize our time, to-do lists, and information. There is so much amazing technology that can help us accomplish these things. At the same time, some people prefer to use paper and pen for organizing. That's fine! I use various cloud-based apps on my computer and phone. I find that the capabilities of these apps far exceed what I can accomplish on paper. I like the convenience of being able to access all my data from any device. I also love knowing that I can't lose it. Even if my computer breaks or I lose my phone, all my data is saved online.

In the following sections, I describe how to use a calendar, project manager, and other information-organizing systems. I also talk about the specific tools that I use. There are many other apps and paper organizers that accomplish similar functions. New digital and physical solutions will come and go; just find the tool that works best for you.

Calendar

Google Calendar helps me keep track of events and organize my day. I can create daily, weekly, monthly, or customized, repeated events. I use this to make *time blocks* on my calendar that reflect my responsibilities, priorities, and goals. For example, I set a goal to write this book because I believed that it would help me accomplish my mission. One of my strategies was to write for six hours a week, so I scheduled two three-hour blocks each week for writing. If I had not blocked off this time, I would not have done it. In fact, I did not write this book for several years after I knew I should because I did not make it a priority on my calendar. Another example is that I take my wife out on a date every Tuesday night. This is a priority, so I have made it an appointment on my calendar. As I process ministry opportunities and other social events, I know that Tuesday nights are not available.

I have most of my week planned out, with time blocks designated for particular activities or responsibilities. One feature I love in Google Calendar is that these blocks can easily be moved by dragging them into other time slots when you need to make adjustments to your day or week (which you will always have to do!). Even though you will have to move your plans around, it is still better to have a plan so that you don't have to spend time during the day thinking of what to do next. With a plan, you can also confidently say no to distractions that come up, because you have your priorities clearly laid out.

The other reason I love Google Calendar is that it is so easy to share with others. Your family, project teams, or staff members can stay on the same page and collaborate efficiently with these shared calendars.

Project and Task Manager

In addition to organizing our time, we also want to organize our projects and tasks. There are some important principles for managing projects and tasks presented in the book *Getting Things Done*, by David Allen. There is an app called Nozbe that is built on the principles in this book (but you don't have read the book to use Nozbe).

I like the fact that Nozbe syncs with Google Calendar and works with Evernote and Google Drive (information and file storage systems). This app is particularly helpful for your project goals.

Information Organization System

I have a file cabinet in the closet in my office. I cannot remember the last time I opened it. I have a few official documents I keep in a fireproof box, but I no longer keep track of information on paper. Today, most of us process the majority of our information digitally. So even if we still have some papers to organize, we need some digital solutions to organizing our information. Here are some apps I use to keep track of general information, habit goals, time use, prayer lists, and finances.

- *Evernote* is a great way to save and organize any notes, thoughts, lists, photos, links, and documents. If you want to create a document with better formatting and outlining capabilities, use *Google Docs.*
- *Way of Life* is a mobile app that helps you track progress with your habit goals. You can create a list of habits you are developing and then categorize and track how well you do each day. This app helps remind you of your habit goals every day and inspires you to keep up with them.
- *ATracker* is a mobile app for keeping track of how you are spending your time. Have you ever been busy all day but felt like you didn't really get anything done? Then you think, *What did I do all day, anyway?* Becoming aware of how we spend our time helps us follow Paul's advice:

  Look carefully then how you walk, not as unwise but as wise, making the best use of the time, because the days are evil.
  Ephesians 5:15–16

  This app can also help you keep track of your goals if you have set a certain amount of time to work on a particular project or responsibility. It can also help you keep up with how many work hours you are putting in. You can create categories and tasks and get detailed data reports on how you have spent your time over days, weeks, or years.
- *PrayerMate* is a mobile app that helps you organize your prayer lists. You can add categories and lists, customize how often certain items appear on your prayer list, and link people to the contacts on your phone.
- *Mint* is a web-based system for keeping up with your finances. You can track all spending with categories and tags, create different accounts, and sync with your bank accounts and credit cards.

Create a Life Plan

Now it's your turn. Set aside some time to pray, and create a life plan! Use these questions to guide the process.

- What is my purpose in life? (Why did God create me?)
- What is my mission?
    - What talents, strengths, desires, and areas of responsibility and influence has God given me?
    - How will I make disciples within my main responsibilities of life: marriage, parenting, church, community, and work?
- What is my vision? (What is it going to look like when I complete the various parts of my mission?)
- What is my passion? (What is at stake? What are the consequences if I do not complete my mission?)
- What are my goals?
    - What must I do to complete my mission in the various aspects of my life?
    - Make sure that your goals are specific and measurable and that they have deadlines.
- What are my strategies? (What must I do to complete each goal?)

After you have created a life plan, then you can follow these steps to begin taking action.

- Make a list of the habit goals you want to accomplish each day or week (or put them in your Way of Life app).
    - Look at this list every day.
    - Keep track of your progress (on a chart or with Way of Life).
- If needed, put on your calendar when you are going to take time to accomplish your habit goals (time with God, exercise, and so forth). You can create a recurring event on Google Calendar.
- If you need regular time blocks to work on your project goals, put them on your calendar.
- Make a list of your projects that require more than one task. Under each project, list the tasks necessary to complete it, and mark the first steps. Make a list of your priority tasks (first steps), or put them on your calendar on the day you want to complete the task. (All of this and much more can be done on Nozbe and Google Calendar.)

- Set a time to review your purpose, mission, passion, vision, goals, projects, tasks, and calendar briefly every day.
- Set a time to review and evaluate your purpose, mission, passion, vision, goals, projects, tasks, and calendar each week. You will need to regularly make adjustments to each of these areas as you pursue your mission.

Discussion Questions

- Why is it important to live with intentionality and resolve?
- Do you have passion? What about?
- Do you set goals regularly?
- Are you an organized person?
- What tools do you use to stay organized?

Big Ideas

- A change of life takes intentionality and resolve.
- Resolutions are decisions we make ahead of time, when we are thinking clearly, that help us stick to it when the going gets tough.
- Our purpose is the reason we exist. Everyone's purpose is the same: God has created us to love him and to love people.
- A mission is something that can be completed. All believers share in the mission God has given us to make disciples of all nations (Matt. 28:18–20).
- Each of us has a unique set of relationships, responsibilities, and abilities that determines the specifics of our mission.
- A passion is more than just a desire. Without passion, we will not have the understanding and strength to say no to our desires.
- Here is what I believe is at stake for all of us:
    - The glory of God.
    - The souls of men.
    - The joy of life.

- A vision is what it looks like when we accomplish our mission.
- Our goals are the concrete steps we must take in order to accomplish our mission.
- Strategies are the specific steps we take and tools we use to accomplish our goals.
- If we are going to live intentionally and accomplish our goals, we will have to stay organized!
- There is so much amazing technology that can help you organize your life. Here are the tools and strategies that I use the most:
  - Google Calendar
  - Nozbe
  - Evernote
  - Way of Life
  - ATracker
  - PrayerMate
  - Mint

APPENDIX A

The Ministry of Giving

How we spend our money is a reflection of our values and priorities and will therefore reflect the lordship of Christ in our lives. Giving a portion of our income is one of the most important ways we acknowledge the lordship of Christ with our possessions. The following statements are principles from the New Testament on giving.

1. The ministry of giving is different than the tithes of the Old Covenant.
   a. The New Testament does not teach believers to tithe.
   b. Most community needs of the Old Covenant for which the tithe was required have been fulfilled or are no longer a part of the community of faith.
   c. Tithing does not fulfill the New Testament teaching on giving (2 Cor. 9:7).
2. The ministry of giving is a privilege from God (2 Cor. 8:1, 4; 9:15; 1 Chron. 29:10–19).
3. The ministry of giving is done willingly (2 Cor. 8:3, 8, 11, 12; 9:2, 5, 7).
4. The ministry of giving is for God's glory (2 Cor. 8:19; 9:7, 11–12, 13; Matt. 6:1–4).
5. The ministry of giving should be cheerful (2 Cor. 9:7).
6. The ministry of giving should be passionate (2 Cor. 8:4, 7, 11; 9:2, 4).
7. The ministry of giving should be generous (2 Cor. 8:2; 9:11, 13)
8. The ministry of giving should be sacrificial (2 Cor. 8:2–3, 9; Luke 21:1–4).

9. The ministry of giving should be in proportion with our supply (2 Cor. 8:3, 12; Luke 12:48).
10. The ministry of giving should be motivated by love (2 Cor. 8:8, 24; 1 Cor. 13:3).
11. The ministry of giving is a blessing to the giver (Acts 20:35; 2 Cor. 8:10; 9:6, 8, 11; Phil. 4:19; Matt. 6:19–20).
12. The ministry of giving includes taking care of those in need (Matt. 5:42, 19:21; 2 Cor. 8:4, 9, 13–15; 9:1, 12; Acts 2:44–45, 4:32–37, 6:1; James 2:15–16; 2 Thess. 3:10–12).
13. The ministry of giving includes supporting ministry.
    a. Local ministers are cared for by the local church (1 Tim. 5:17; Gal. 6:6).
    b. Sent ministers, like missionaries, are also supported by local churches (2 Cor. 11:8–9; Phil. 4:14–16).
    c. Those in ministry (often specifically elders) are not to be seeking personal gain through their service (Acts 20:33–35; 1 Tim. 3:3; 6:5, 8; Titus 1:7, 11; 1 Pet. 5:21; 1 Tim. 6:5).
    d. A direct link between ministry and material support can be an obstacle to the gospel (1 Cor. 9:12; 2 Cor. 11:7; 1 Thess. 2:9; 2 Thess. 3:7–8).
14. The ministry of giving is done individually and corporately (Matt. 5:42, 19:21; 2 Cor. 11:7–11; Phil. 4:14–16).
    a. Examples of giving in the NT indicate that, when believers gave corporately, they were giving to a particular need or types of needs (Acts 2:44–45, 4:32–37, 6:1; 1 Cor. 16:1–4; 2 Cor. 9:1, 5).
    b. Believers who receive financial support from the church have certain qualifications (1 Tim. 5:3–16; 2 Thess. 3:6–12).
    c. Corporate funds are handled with integrity and accountability (1 Cor. 16:3–4).

These principles should guide individual and corporate ministries of giving, but you are going to have to work out the details. As you read these passages, think and pray through how God would have you give. Although the New Testament does not teach believers to tithe, it does teach that the ministry of giving should be in proportion with our supply. Therefore, it makes sense to choose to give a particular percentage of your income. Since *tithe* generally means "a tenth," many believers give a minimum of 10 percent of their income as a beginning point for their giving.

APPENDIX B

A Scripture Memory Review System

—∞—

To begin your Scripture Memory Review System, choose a book, chapter, or passage you would like to memorize. It is better to memorize large sections of Scripture so that you can understand its context. However, this review system works for short verses, too.

Day 1: Memorize the First Verse

1. Read the first verse five times (or seven or ten, depending on your need). As you do this, be sure that you do the following:
   a. Include the verse numbers (say "two three" for 2:3). This will become helpful for recall and ministry.
   b. Consider the meaning of the verse. Read it out loud in a way that expresses its meaning.
   c. Visually photograph the words, or create images of its meaning in your mind. You may also find it helpful to write out the verse by hand.
2. Repeat the first verse aloud five times (or seven or ten) without looking.

Day 2: Review and Memorize

1. Review the verse you memorized yesterday. Repeat it five times without looking. Don't forget to do these things:

   a. Include the verse numbers.
   b. Consider the meaning of the verse, and say it out loud in a way that expresses the meaning.
2. Memorize the next verse as described in Day 1.

Day 3: Review and Memorize

1. Review the verse you memorized yesterday. Repeat it five times without looking. Don't forget to do the following:
   a. Include the verse numbers.
   b. Consider the meaning of the verse, and say it out loud in a way that expresses the meaning.
2. Repeat one time all the verses you have memorized together.
3. Memorize the next verse as described in Day 1.

Day 4 (and After): Review and Memorize

1. Repeat what is described in Day 3 until you complete the passage or chapter.
2. Once completed, put the passage on your Daily Scripture Memory Review chart, and review it for fourteen days.
3. Then place the passage on your Weekly Scripture Memory Review chart, and review it once a week for seven weeks.
4. Then place the passage on your Monthly Scripture Memory Review chart, and review it once a month for the rest of your life!

Daily Procedure

1. Continue to review and memorize the passage you are currently working on, as described in Day 3.

2. Review all the passages on your daily chart.
    a. This will normally only be one or two passages, depending on how many you are trying to memorize at once.
3. Review a passage from your weekly chart.
    a. You won't have to do this every day unless you have around seven passages on this chart.
4. Review a passage from your monthly chart.
    a. You can do this during other daily activities: showering, driving, waiting, cleaning, or exercising. Make it a part of your daily routine.
    b. You won't have to do this every day unless you have around thirty passages on this chart.

Scripture Memory Review

Daily

Reference	1	2	3	4	5	6	7	8	9	10	11	12	13	14

WEEKLY

Reference	1	2	3	4	5	6	7

Monthly

Reference	J	F	M	A	M	J	J	A	S	O	N	D

APPENDIX C

Word Studies from 2 Timothy 3:16

All Scripture is breathed out by God and profitable
for teaching, for reproof, for correction, and for training in righteousness,
that the man of God may be complete, equipped for every good work.
2 Timothy 3:16–17

As we study 2 Timothy 3:16, we will notice the list of activities for which Scripture is profitable: *teaching*, *reproof*, *correction*, and *training*. Two Bible study questions we may ask are: How are these terms different from one another, and how do they relate to each other?

By using an exhaustive concordance, interlinear Bible, or Bible software, we will be able to identify the Greek words from which these English words are translated. You can find several free interlinear Bibles online. In the list below, the English word is followed by the transliteration of the Greek in English letters.

- Teaching *didaskalia*
- Reproof *elegmos*
- Correction *epanorthosis*
- Training *paideia*

Now we can use *Mounce's Complete Expository Dictionary* (*MED*) to find out more about their meanings. One quick piece of advice: carefully read *MED*'s "Two Ways to Use This Book" and "How to Do Word Studies" before you try to use this resource on your own.[15] As an experienced Bible student, I thought

I could figure it out, but I couldn't. This does not mean this resource is hard to use; it just means that you have to understand how it works to use it well. Using a tool like this may seem overwhelming, but be encouraged: anyone who is serious about studying the Bible can use it!

Teaching

When we look up *teaching* in *MED*, we find two Greek words listed under the New Testament section. The first one, *didaskalia*, is the one that appears in 2 Timothy 3:16, and "denotes 'teaching' or 'doctrine,' both the content and the act." The other words listed with *teaching* in 2 Timothy 3:16 also indicate acts, so we can assume that *didaskalia* refers to the act of teaching doctrine.

Reproof

When we look up *reproof* in *MED*, we read, "See *rebuke*." Under the entry for *rebuke*, the Greek word we are looking for, *elegmos*, is not listed. This is when another section of *MED*, the Greek–English dictionary at the back of the book, is helpful. You will notice that it follows the Greek alphabet, not the English. So if you look on page x of the Greek transliterations, you will find the order of the Greek alphabet.

In this dictionary, we discover that *elegmos* appears only in 2 Timothy 3:16, and it simply means "reproof." It is also "a later equivalent to *elenchos*."[16] *Elenchos* is "a trial in order to proof, a proof."[17] We know that in English, *rebuke* and *reproof* indicate a disapproval or correction of something.

Correction

There are no New Testament words listed under the entry for *correction*. In the Greek–English dictionary, we once again find that *epanorthosis* only appears here in the New Testament. It means "correction, reformation, improvement."[18]

Training

Training does not appear in the expositor dictionary section. In the Greek–English dictionary, *paideia* means "instruction, discipline" in 2 Timothy 3:16.[19]

Observations

As we already observed from the English translation, there is a lot of overlap in the meanings of these words. We may notice that the first and last words, *teaching* and *training*, have a more positive, instructional meaning than the other two. *Reproof* and *correction* both indicate the presence of something wrong or false that must be made right.

As we look for other overlaps or relationships, it seems that *teaching* is more related to doctrine and *training* more to behavior. The meaning for *correction*, with ideas such as "reformation" and "improvement," also seem to relate more to behavior than doctrine. Not only does there seem to be a relationship between these words, but a pattern may be emerging:

- "Teaching" refers to instruction in correct doctrine.
- "Reproof" refers to correction of false doctrine.
- "Correction" refers to correction of wrong behavior.
- "Training" refers to instruction in right behavior.

This kind of pattern is common in Paul's writings. As we read commentaries and continue studying this passage, we can further test the accuracy of these observations.

APPENDIX D

Recommended Resources

Alcorn, Randy. 2003. *Money, Possessions and Eternity.* Carol Stream, Illinois: Tyndale House Publishers. (A smaller book with similar material is Alcorn's *Managing God's Money.*)

Allen, David. 2001. *Getting Things Done: The Art of Stress-Free Productivity.* London: Penguin Books.

Anderson, Neil T. 2000. *The Bondage Breaker: Overcoming Negative Thoughts, Irrational Feelings, Habitual Sins.* Eugene, Oregon: Harvest House Publishers.

Baucham, Voddie. 2004. *The Ever-Loving Truth: Can Faith Thrive in a Post-Christian Culture?* Nashville: Broadman & Holman Publishers.

Blackaby, Henry T. and Claude V. King. 2005. *Experiencing God: Student Edition.* Nashville: LifeWay Press.

Bonhoeffer, Dietrich. 1995. *The Cost of Discipleship.* New York: Touchstone (first published in 1937).

Covey, Stephen R. 1994. *First Things First.* New York: Simon & Schuster.

Eastman, Dick. 1978. *The Hour That Changes the World: A Practical Plan for Personal Prayer.* Grand Rapids: Baker Books.

Frizzell, Gregory. 1999. *How to Have a Powerful Prayer Life: The Biblical Path to Holiness and Relationship with God.* Memphis: The Master Design.

_____. 2000. *Returning to Holiness: A Personal and Churchwide Journey to Revival.* Memphis: The Master Design.

Geisler, Norman and Frank Turek. 2004. *I Don't Have Enough Faith to Be an Atheist.* Wheaton, Illinois: Crossway Books.

Hindson, Ed and Elmer L. Towns. 2013. *Illustrated Bible Survey: An Introduction.* Nashville: B&H Publishing Group.

Lewis, C. S. 1980. *Mere Christianity.* New York: Macmillan Publishing Company.

McDill, Wayne. 2006. *12 Essential Skills for Great Preaching*, 2nd ed. Nashville: B&H Publishing Group.

_____. 2010. *Making Friends for Christ: A Practical Approach to Relational Evangelism*, 2nd ed. USA, Xulon Press.

Mounce, William D. 2006. *Mounce's Complete Expository Dictionary of Old and New Testament Words.* Grand Rapids: Zondervan.

Thomas, Gary. 2000. *Sacred Marriage: What If God Designed Marriage to Make Us Holy More Than to Make Us Happy?* Grand Rapids: Zondervan.

Tripp, Tedd. 2005. *Shepherding a Child's Heart*, 2nd ed. Wapwallopen, PA: Shepherd Press.

Whitney, Donald S. 2015. *Praying the Bible.* Wheaton, Illinois: Crossway.

ABOUT THE AUTHOR

—ꟾ—

DR. MATTHEW MCDILL HAS SERVED in pastoral ministry for the last twenty years. He is currently a pastor of Highland Christian Fellowship in Boone, North Carolina, which he helped to start in 2005. Through his ministry, Truth to Freedom, he teaches and writes about discipleship, marriage, family, parenting, home education, and church. He holds a bachelor's degree in communication and two master's degrees and a doctorate in biblical studies. Matthew and his wife, Dana, homeschool their nine children in Creston, North Carolina.

NOTES

1. Here are six scientific observations you can study more to learn how they point to a Creator: 1. the order of the universe (the teleological argument); 2. the existence of DNA; 3. the impossibility of spontaneous generation; 4. the second law of thermodynamics; 5. the gene pool and the limits to change; 6. fossil gaps and intermediate forms.

2. Randy Alcorn, *Money, Possessions and Eternity* (Carol Stream, Illinois: Tyndale House Publishers, 2003), 5.

3. Gregory Frizzell, *How to Have a Powerful Prayer Life: The Biblical Path to Holiness and Relationship with God* (Memphis: The Master Design, 1999), 17, 19.

4. Ibid., 8.

5. William D. Mounce, *Mounce's Complete Expository Dictionary of Old and New Testament Words* (Grand Rapids: Zondervan, 2006), xiii.

6. Ibid., 13.

7. Ibid., 33.

8. Ibid., 51.

9. Wayne McDill, *Making Friends for Christ: A Practical Approach to Relational Evangelism*, 2nd ed. (USA: Xulon Press, 2010), 35, 36.

10. Ibid., 56.

11. Ibid., 102.

12. Ibid., 126–27.

13. Ted Tripp includes a similar chart in his book. Ted Tripp, *Shepherding a Child's Heart*, 2nd ed. (Wapwallopen, PA: Shepherd Press, 2005), 201.

14. Henry T. Blackaby and Claude V. King, *Experiencing God: Student Edition* (Nashville: LifeWay Press, 2005), 170.

15. Mounce, *Mounce's Complete Expository Dictionary*, xi, xiii.

16. Ibid., 1139

17. Ibid., 1139.

18. Ibid., 1149.

19. Ibid., 1230.

Made in the USA
Lexington, KY
14 June 2018